KENNETH BERNARD DEAN

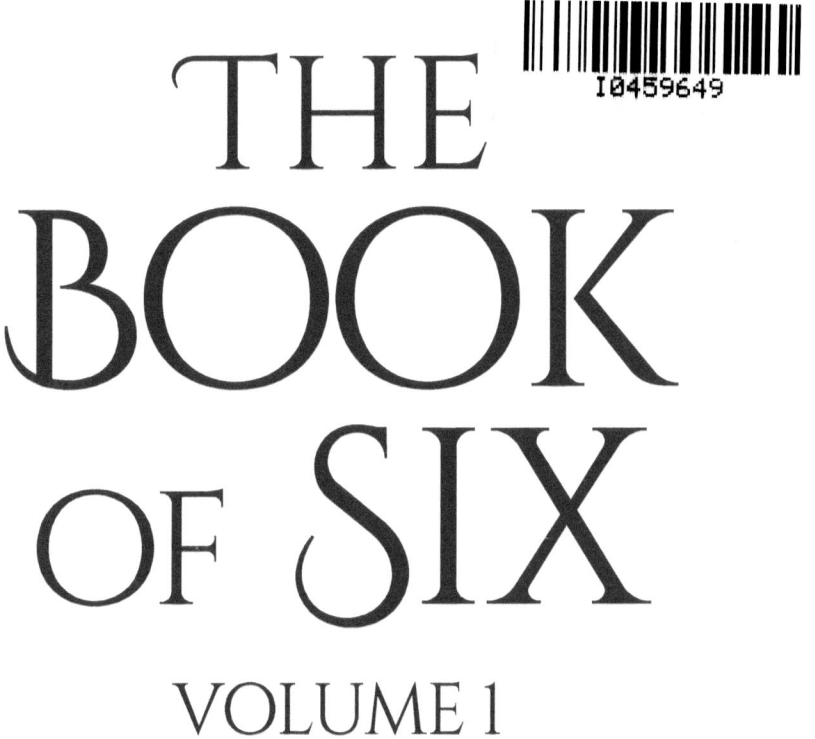

THE BOOK OF SIX

VOLUME 1

WHAT LIES IN
THE MIND OF INSANITY
NEW EDITION

ISBN: 979-8-89216-027-8 (Paperback)

Library of Congress Control Number: 2024914322

BookmarcAlliance
California, USA
www.bookmarcalliance.com

TABLE OF CONTENTS

PRELUDE FOR VOLUME 1

What Lies in the Mind of Insanity

The Book of Six is an open mind share, meant to rekindle that thing inside, which makes us both humanly open to or curiously in search of the truth. Now some of you may consider that to be somewhat a bold, and overly confident statement to make. Yet there are those who might even consider it to be blasphemy, thus that is something that perhaps even you might contemplate once you've read the contents of the eight pieces totaling about 41,216 words, which I have chosen to release at this point and now.

I guess the answer if questioned, "Why now would you decide to write something, which is so far from what the belief of the system should be, are you the one we should fear?" "I mean those words you scribe; we have not seen or worried over them for many centuries now!" "For it has been said in the times to come, when all things must come full circle." "These things would be scribed that no one, can claim ignorance to truth." "Is it true, have we finally come full circle?" These are just a few of the many questions, which vexes my mind as the mood surrounds me, like a sweet fragrance refreshing the atmosphere, while death linger about in many forms. Yet in my heart, the only answer that is true (I guess) would be, the questions above all is my reason or perhaps my purpose. For that is my purpose, to please that which gave concept, and purpose that I may live to serve Him!

This is not just the daydreams, nightdreams or even the conversations between the Lord God, and me that is in documentation here. But the words I've been told to scribe by him. "Do I have control over what it is, I'm told to scribe?" "No, I don't!" Moreover, there can be no rest, till such time as the task is done."

However, I'm both Grateful, and Humbled the Lord didn't just cast me down here and without purpose. Thus, I shall forever do his bidding as a scribe, also I shall worship (with faith liken to steel) him eternally. For I am SIX, the one he chose to scribe his words that you might be gifted by their gift of wisdom. So, without further ado, I give you "The Book of SIX vol.1 What lies in the mind of insanity" by Kenneth Bernard Dean/LDD/Six. There are eight stories. The first one is titled "Change, a look within the mind of insanity," this is a short story of 13,558 words, which I hope will explain the way in which I think. Also perhaps you might find that in some ways, the way we both think is not so different after all. The second one is titled "Council before the Great Almighty on the Subject of Man," which is a 4,456 word short story which I think you'll enjoy. For the journey which it takes you on, is one which may have you question your purpose here on this world Earth. So, with that all being said, I only ask that you, while reading the material, please do it with an open mind.

The third story is titled, " It is what it is," though it is of only 793 words, I believe that once you have read and understood its purpose. I know that you will be surprised of the impact it throws at you.

The forth story is titled "The Art of Life," and is a 3,743 word short story of a simple procrastination in which I'll let you be the judge of its contents, for in many ways perhaps even you've entertained same or similar procrastinations as well, do you not think or believe it to be so? Then there is the fifth story of the book, which is one of imagination; for it is a story where upon, I cast myself into the lead character as we together endure the plot of it all. The name of this story is "The Man Name Six" and it is a 4,217 word story set to trigger even your thoughts of who, and what I am; as well as you also.

Thus, we come to story number six, and the title of this one is "Three short stories" of 11,735 words combined, and the three titles are: "A Time Before Time, How it really was, and Still Is," "What came first, the chicken or the egg," and the last of the three is "The Birth of the Man Child," this is like a small book in itself. Alonge with the many turns it will take you on the hope is that you will enjoy all three of them. The next story is "True Salt," a short 1,036 word story of what it might have been like, for the Lord God once He (in fact) did create the first of many humanoid male creations. For it, in some ways, speak to perhaps the joy shared by them both as they ran barefooted across the worlds globe, as they both play catch-me, catch-me, and with the placing of each of their feet; thus, the great gardens of the world came to be. A rather fun read with many angles of joy to take in; while at the same time acquiring the hidden message, covertly placed within the mist of it all. However, the last of the eight stories is titled "What is the Price for life," a 1,678 word short story. Which is really about understanding the true worth of this gift call life, as well as some pointers on how best to show appreciation for this gift as well.

Also, I ask that if you find that the material is appealing to your sense of curiosity, and question of what is or is not the truth, and you want more then contact me by way of my email address and let me direct you where you can find more of my books to stimulate the curiosity which lie within your need to appease your open-mindedness. Again, thank you, and like always the hope is that you enjoy.

Thank you,
Kenneth Bernard Dean/LDD/Six
forwardtodelta@yahoo.com

CHAPTER 1

Change, a look within the mind of insanity

~Author's Words~

The things that I am about to write about, are what I perceive true change in a person to be. Though, the fact that these things' that I am about to write, are of my own personal experience. Keep in mind that though some may find it hard to think anything other than, this view of change to be of a one sided point of view nature. However, still as you the reader, read on, I am sure that you will agree that the similarities may or may not be of great important after all. For as we together explore this thing that we call "Change, a look within the mind of insanity," and how it relate to our individuality in the whole of things. Moreover, our focus should be on the "Guarantee!" For that alone should be, all that matters once one realizes how awaken he or she really is. Thus, acquiring a glimpse or sense of their true purpose and or prime directive.

I guess what I am asking is that you (the reader), attacks this statement of "Change in the person" with a veracity, and a great hunger for real understanding and real truth. Whether it is yours or someone else's hope for this great knowledge and truth. The manner of which to measure the change in your own self, is the key to perhaps achieving both the Knowledge, as well as that Truth that we are all so seeking to find. Even if but, to maybe maintain what little positive self-change and sanity, you may have already acquired. Therefore, with no further ado, I give to you "Change, a look within the mind of insanity." Also like always, I truly hope that you (the reader), will both take something positive from it, as well as enjoy it...

CHANGE, A LOOK WITHIN THE MIND OF INSANITY

Chapter 1: How it all came about

"What is the biggest fear, which plagues' your concept for change within you. Is it the fear of not being true to change or the fear that you won't be able to measure up to the standard set, for said changes?" Then come journey with me, through the darkness of my venture. Then ask yourself again, those same questions. For by the end of the read, I can assure you that your answer will be quite different from the ones that you are already pondering now…

As far back as I can remember, there was always a thing in me. Which always had me question, whatever choices I made. Thoughts would come to me, as if to question whether or not I had looked at all of the available options when I chose as I did.

In addition the question of *"Could I have done things differently,"* was the one curse that plagued me, for pretty much the whole of my life. It was almost like; I would try to console myself by saying that this is all I have to choose from. For I am called nigger, and when you are called nigger. The only good choices that are available, are the ones that no one else wants.

Thus, the only things' or choices that was left. Were the bad to worse choices no one else wanted. Thus, that is all I had. However, had I tried just a little harder, to see through the lies. Then perhaps the truth (that being) better choices, would have been revealed to me. In addition, if all those forced to believe that most powerful lie of *"That is all we have to choose from,"* perhaps would have also made even better choices in their lives as well. Then maybe life would have been better for not just us, but our victims as well. Oh yes, I did say victims because with every choice that we make in life, somebody wins and someone else loses. Thus, the title of victim is always given to the loser. *"Why is it, you might ask?"* Thus, the answer is because, they became a victim of said choices you made. Thus in a sense, you must have chosen right. However, in reality that truly is not the case.

For, in that situation or in the real world. Both parties are victims, and they both lose. *"Why is this, you might ask again?"*

Well, at this time in the game, the only answer is because of the one for making a bad choice, and the other because of the bad choice! Then there was a period in which, I could not stand to be in front of a mirror or to see my reflection on any surface because of those choices that I had made.

Though I am not as handsome, as most people that exist that was not the case, However, it was my outer light that was the problem. You know that light, which perceives you in life, is what had me so afraid.

For my reflection, had become so cold that it took away from the brightness, and the warmth of that light so gifted unto me, and by way of my creator.

Thus, it left ice-cold hate, and death in the eyes of me. This bearer of such a heavy burden, the one burden I know to be self-made. Now this went on for quite some time, and as the days passed. I thought only of this, and how it was affecting me along with, my place in society. In addition, it spun thoughts of how best I could better myself. Thus making me, a proper citizen in the society.

Nevertheless, as I learned further down the way in life, there is no such thing as outside change. For if a person wishes to change. They must do it first from within their mindset, if ever to make a difference.

Like the one so talked about, you know *the proper citizen in the society thing.* Thus, I embarked on a quest, to find the way in which, first to identify what change would look or feel like. Then next, to locate these characteristic within myself. But to no avail.

For, no one ever told me that the process of change, had to be timed into your needs before it could be even requested.

So now I am confronted with a *"How do I, solve this problem?"* situation, and for once I guess I can say, I was truly lost. I even considered giving up on this thing call *Change*, and maybe even go back to the way things were in the past. Before the thought of a *Change*, even came to mind.

Okay hear me on this and think heavy on the answer if you do not mind. Now speaking from a spiritual point of view, have you ever been touched? You know touched? Yet, when you turned around to see whom it might be, you find that there is no one there. Sort of like, the seed is planted therefore, you just go along like a robot under control, just toiling with whatever new thing it is, you were pursuing.

Some call it, the moment when the Deity steps in, and touch you with a good spirit. More or less like, he makes the choice for you, and you follow through with it. Thus, I guess was the case with me, nonetheless. I mean, keep in mind that the process, was one that would span a period, of about thirty years plus.

Now during this period, the only things I was privy to, was to be focused on making the right choices in life first, and the other one was to survive. For to neglect to do the first one first (that being to make right choices throughout life, and in direct accordance with, the laws that govern that process), would surely cause my death. As it did in the year of 1983, and the date was the 10th of March.

Although they were successful in their endeavor, of bringing me back from death, while on route to the morgue after three days. This death would only serve to make me aware of the concept of the different dimensions of life. Yet alternatively, perhaps it should have also made me aware of my need for change in my life. But now I know that in my life (when I look back), and during that time it was not to be. At least not just yet! I mean, for a person like me to change. I would have to experience, the whole of the world completely, and then survive it.

First, and most importantly. I had to experience death, and this would prove to be, the one great tool in my arsenal for change. Moreover, when change finally do come that tool would help, to keep me focused. By allowing me to see the other side, and to remember the severity, of the consequences for the choice made.

Now, this would prove to be also, quite important in the change process. Thus, on March 10, 1983. The day of my death was also, the day of my rebirth, an all in one thing. It was like, I had to experience the world of death for three days, and nights before the rebirth took place. Now I know that there are those, who would first read this far in the piece, then say in a loud voice *"This is bullshit!"* Thus the reason is because, how many of those individuals has the Lord the Deity took under his wings. Thus allowing them to experience, what it is I have experienced. Or to see life from both side of reality, like the one venture I was allowed to experience (that being death). So this is the reason why, I know this to be truly true. Moreover, it allows me to without fear, write this for you!

"Well, what did you gain, from this great experience?" Is the question most asked, and by those lucky enough to know me. Seeking both the knowledge gained from that venture, and knowledge of things that I went through, over thirty years ago, which resulted in me being murdered. So I say to them, "In the consequence, of the choice I made that day, is what holds that answer."

However, the only thing that I could feel for them, was contempt. For the future, and change was never revealed to them. So how do you explain something like, what I had to go through, and in a way in which, they would understand it? Like what words do I use, and what manner do I speak to them in. So as, not to come off to bold or self-invested.

Moreover, it had become clear to me that this, was a "no-can-do" thing! Like, the kind of thing that you know. But you do not tell or let anyone know that you know! For to do so, surely would lead up to them attempting to lock you in that place. You know that place, where they put those, they do not understand.

They have been known, to even tell the world that this may be a sickness. Moreover, like where you are is for medical reasons or perhaps for some medical testing of course! Therefore, I just kept it to myself in thought. But, as far as in the eyes of those around me. I could see, they thought of me, as a possible mere mark. Now, truly that is not a good thing, for that was to be there biggest mistake. Thus like an angler, I would cast that look to them. I mean, it was as if they were fish, and my presents were an angler's hook. I mean to no amazement to me, like hungry fish in an early day breeze. They would always bite, and I would always reel them in.

In addition, I was riding just under the radar of their awareness. So it allowed me, to do things that they themselves, may have thought was beyond reproach.

Things like, extracting information from street level thugs, who themselves were not too smart. For, they thought of me as a mark to city, and government level employee. However, what these fools failed to get. Was that from these city, and government employees, is where I got my best information from. The kind of information about criminal activity, throughout the perspective many town's or cities in which, this process of change within me, was to take place. While all the time still doing my thing, which was crime.

Look you might ask me, "*Well, how could that be possible?*" So all I can say, is that when the Lord the Deity touches someone, there is a mark that is placed upon that individuals head. Thus, when someone comes in contact with that person, they gravitate unwillingly to them. In addition, they listen to everything, which that person has to say as if it is the law. Like euphorically, they become a slave to each, and every word that comes from their mouth.

Thus in a sense, though the Lord had touched me, there was still that evilness, embedded deep within that was still a part of life for me. Plus the only way it came out, was in that way, and at those people or should I say victims. For, I had come to be known to them as *UNCLE!* However, they never knew what that really stood for. I mean in truth, they had lent themselves over to me, and my experience of the process of change. Yet, never did anyone question, what *UNCLE* stood for. Or what affect that knowledge would have on their future. Moreover, what it would take, for them to even change or even be cleansed from the evilness, which they had so been confronted with. It was like they had become, these "*Men from UNCLE crime family members,*" and with me at the top. But all I wanted, was to properly change and completely. Still all they would ask is, *"Why do you want to change?"* that is when it became clear, they had not a clue as to what was happening, to either myself or even them. For in that moment alone. They had surrendered themselves, to the wills of my evil concept on life itself. For, they strongly considered each word, like sheep. As I was casting them out, and reeling them back, from within a world, from which it all came.

However, it must have been for some purpose, but what purpose, I cannot say. Also, telling you about it over again will not help. Because, as you read this, and hopefully understand; that it is written by the hand, of a person who has died many times. Only to be brought back to complete, this process of change that comes from within. Less you ever understand or grasp those basic points first. Chances are, you will never ever fully understand what it is, I am conveying or trying to convey to you. As being the truth, as I experienced it.

Look, there are or never was any barrier, which I could not overcome. Why? Because, the Lord the Deity, had his mark upon me. Now, when it is like that nothing can touch you. For, to lay hands upon one that holds the mark upon, his or her head. Would invite great retaliation, from the Lord the Deity himself! A fate, which no one really live to talk about. Even mercy, for such a thing, is known to leave them usually mindless shells or vegetables in a hospital room somewhere.

Now, you may think, there is a sense of bragging on my behalf. But actually all I am doing, is giving you the situation as it was, and the way I now see it to be.

So trust me when I say, as you read further all this that you have read so far. Will help with the understanding, of what it was like for me, and those around me. In addition, how the Lord the Deity would manifest himself to me, and what it was like.

Or being in both his presence, and still being yourself seeking only understanding. While during those times of transitional changes, both inside and out was quite unusual, as well as eye opening in a way!

CHANGE, A LOOK WITHIN THE MIND OF INSANITY

Chapter 2: The gift within

There was once a man, who the people referred to as "the touched one," in a town to the north. Now, what they did not know, was that he was in fact touched, and by the Lord the Deity. For upon the head of the man, was indeed a mark. One that only, those touched in such a manner, would be blessed to ware, or see.

Now, in the early hours of one night, and earlier that week. I was awoken, and asked to go to that particular little town, and seek out this man. Thus, this I did do. But why, one might ask? Because when the Lord the Deity speaks to you, you do not ask questions, you just go, or you just do. Thus this I did do, and upon finding the town, I soon found the man as well. It then dawned on me. That I knew not the purpose, of my being there or what I was to say (if anything), to this man.

But as I looked closer to this man, and into his eyes (even though the many could not), I could see that he was gifted, and with the gift of the mark upon his head. This mark of the Lord, the Deity. Then this person of the gift, asked me if I knew or could see; that he was in fact, the one that was truly touched by the Lord the Deity. So I said yes. Then he got up, came to me, and placed one of his hands upon my forehead, and the other over the crown of my head. Then the Lord the Deity came and manifested his self into the man. Thus I fell into slumber, and when I was awoke. I also had the gift, which is the mark upon my head also, and the Lord the Deity now will be with me forever until the end of time itself …

There comes a time in the life of the gifted ones, when they began to maybe, understand what it is which is upon them. Though it happens, it is only by the choice or way of this, the Lord the Deity. Thus, it would occur, and for his pleasure only. However, for the rest. This understanding is gradual, and for good reason. Because in order for the individual to ever get the maximum knowledge and understanding of the lesson. They must first live it every step of the journey, and while carrying the mark of the Lord the Deity, upon their head.

I mean, there was things that I did, and even I knew that at the least. I should have died, if not landed in prison for the remainder of my days. Nevertheless, due to the fact his wings were around me, and because of the mark that he (himself) had placed upon me. It allowed me, not to be touched by the laws, as well as the hands of man. For they (to me), did not matter anymore. Plus all that lay before me now, was part of whatever concept of a lesson, he had for me to learn!

Now there are those that will say, *WHY YOU?* Well all I can say is, because at the time of my greatest despair, and while in the mist of the darken night. Like during the times, when I suffered along with the pain, and agony of being a boy of five or maybe less, while being abused psychologically from society, and the American culture, along with being beaten to the point of a close too death state I would call out to him and ask the question of "*Why would anyone, ever be allowed to do this to me?*" Then often I would ask myself, "*is this my purpose, and if so, why is it that I should suffer so?*" In addition, the answer always was because many times mom got in the zone somewhat, as if she really enjoyed those beating that she gave me. So for a while, I was able to pass the blame onto the shoulders of her.

You know, I do not even think that she even realized what it was that she was doing, for when I look back on it all it becomes vividly clear that she, herself was battling with her own fears and demons of despair. *YES!* Through it all, I think he, the Lord, heard my cry for mercy, and death as well as hers. Moreover my hopes were of being once again, back with him the way it was in the pass, long before this world even existed long before I so gallantly took upon the test of trials and tribulations for him alone.

Now that is when I believe, he decided I would be perfect for his experiment, the one called life. Thus the relationship that came from that moment to this day still exists, and it must be for something more than just, trivial human ego or the joys of a creator, why? Because in that moment the pain that was upon me somehow dissipated, and for a short moment I could feel the presents of his comfort about me as if being wrapped in a warm blanket of love and safety.

However, enough with that, and let us back up for just a little. Because from that kind of conditioning I now understand and remember that in my heart there was no love, less it was for the love of pain and not man or the other entities which co-existed within his domain. So for me to show actually someone or for that matter even myself love, was again one of those *"no can do things."*

However, keep in mind that I had the great gift of gab, and if any ear were exposed to my voice and the words there of, then the owner of that ear was soon to be somewhat enslaved by both the words, and the manner in which they were spoken. For I had the belief that this was my calling; Clearly, I could not have been closer to the truth, but with a twist. For while I toyed with perfecting my ability of the art of control through words, it took me off the path of self-pity, and allowed me to experience true power of wealth without the tangibility of hard treasure like fine linen cloth, silks, and metals like gold, silver, platinum or the rarest of the sort after stones like diamonds, rubies or emeralds.,

In a sense, my awareness for what was my purpose or even where in the spectrum of this existence I might be place if even, had in a way became both clear and with reason for my existence. This then became the answer to the question so many times before I had asked myself, which in that moment it began to change the whole of me. In addition to my amazement, there were times when I would find myself able to cross over into the perspective adjacent dominions. Now understand that in the next few minutes, I am going to reveal things to you (the reader), which I have not ever been able to reveal to anyone.

You will be walked into the worlds of reality that not only exist but exist in real time in a co-existing state for me. Now, even though it is against the laws of creativity, and physic for them to ever cross over and have contact in real time, yet these things I was allowed to experience. Did I question what was going on at the time, yes, I did. But there was a sense of surreal tranquility, and peace like I had never felt before. Like for once I was safe and free from the pain and chaos that had so controlled my life; moreover there, there was love, a love that can only be explained as being of God himself.

For unlike you, no longer was I in the eyes of the Lord the Deity, considered just simple human any longer. For he, the Deity, had placed hands upon my head, and left me with his mark. So now, at least my father had taken an interest in me (his son), and for once I can truly say that I felt real love. You know the kind that protect, as well as teach. I mean face it; I was his experiment. Laid out before his angelic counsel, in the hope of bearing the truth before them, that they might see that he is the true Almighty.

CHANGE, A LOOK WITHIN
THE MIND OF INSANITY

Chapter 3: The process of change/the experiment

For what purpose will this process of change serve in this experiment? For our question is one of being elevated to the status of creator, a status liken only to you Lord.

Well then, my son Lucifer, you shall find this most challenging, and to the rest very much informing, thus bring forth the Man creation, thus entered in me the experiment.

And as I walked in, and bared my presents before them, the sounds of that moment from the angelic counsel became loud in the perfect pitch of praise, and glory.

For the long awaited test of the trials and tribulation for the Almighty, was soon to be brought before for all to watch and experience!

Now as I remember back to the first time that I was able to cross over into another dominion, I recall that it was like the most vivid acid trip ever known to man. I mean the colors, smells, and the creatures themselves were like opening a door to a studio set at Hollywood, California Dream-works studios. However, you would have thought that they might be frightened by my presents, but that was not the case. It was as if they knew that I was to be there at that time, and they had no problem what so ever with it.

Again the question comes up *"Why?,"* but only because there was an even deeper answer to be sot within me, and by me. Moreover,

I soon was informed that these creatures were the products and equations, of many lessons as well as of many experiments for which, to educate the angelic counsel of the Deity.

Plus it also came about with the request of favors from the Deity himself. For this was the place, where we would all come together, and just be in a sense young people, and do the things that young people do, without persecution from anyone. You know, for the first time in my life, I felt like a person, a kid, and one who could for once actually smile.

During those moments, my heart was at peace, a peace like none that I ever felt before, and I had friends, many friends; grant it they were not like what you would expect, as far as appearance. However, still friends, nonetheless. These friends were animals, and insect that could speak. Elf's and Gnome's that had great intellect and the surrounding view was one of vast beauty, and vivid colors.

There was a boy no bigger than a mouse, but with the gift of flight added to his DNA structure, it allowed him, and his people to compete on their world. I mean, there was more than I could ever imagine, and they were all as real as I was!

Another time there was this place or dominion that I went to, that reminded me so much of what the book of words describe as to be, the appearance of what hell might both, be like, and look like. Nevertheless, the people were quiet kind, and reserved to doing good things for each other, unlike the way it is here on earth. Now keep in mind that, these journeys were a way for me to download, plus to look at the way others live socially, and to pick from their ways those things that would help me, to survive on my own world as well as any of theirs…

Now in the morning that followed the big slumber, the day was much like many to come, and I had just come from this dominion, which I like to call midway world. The temperature, it must have been ninety degrees at the lowest, and the lesson for the day was one of choice so that everybody victim, and perpetrator alike, come out on the winning end.

Sounds very easy (do it not?); however this would prove to be one of my greatest works, second only to the day that I was shot to death. For I was learning, the art of selling a dream as if it was the real deal.

Therefore, like most day's back then, I just went the way in which I always did. Which mean, I was out on the prowl like a hungry beast, looking for pray thus was the way. Soon, there it was in all its "pleasing glory, my pray" that is. Therefore, as I approached him, it was like a work in progress.

As I spoke, my voice seems to have captured his attention, as he moved my way answering with something like, *"Can you help me bro?"* My view of him was like looking into the eyes of a sheep wanting to be slaughtered. There for like most beast of pray, I took my time sizing this fresh new feast up, for the pleasure of no one but me. I mean the thought of, if he had a family of people who loved, and depended on him for survival, really did not come into play. It was as if I did not care, and to the point that if they were there, they themselves were as good as gone as well.

"My nigger what-up, do you need something? How much do you want to spend?" … *"Well I'm working with fifty for now, but if it's good stuff then, I'll really spend!"* … *"Okay, you got a car?"* … *"Yeah, but it's my girls, and she does not know what I do"* … *"Well then she'll never hear it from me, oh by the way you got a stem?"* … *"Yeah!"* … *"Okay then when we get in the car, I got some stuff with me, and you can try it before you buy, cool?"* … *"Alright!"* …

Therefore, with that we climbed into his girlfriend's car, and like promised. I gave him a piece to try, when he lit, and pulled the smoke of that white death down into his lungs. I knew that he was my feast for the night, cash, car, and all; "Hum!" with even a bit more persuasion to his mind, I knew that he could be turned, and would wear my mark upon his mind, thus even subjecting him to die for me if asked.

I mean face it! I was in beast mode, and when it's like that, all that come in contact with me, are pray or victims. Cold hearted, NO! Survival, Yes! Why, because that is what I was. Like that boogieman many people tell their children about, well I was it in the living flesh of man, and right now I had a mission, and he was sitting right next to me, in his girlfriend's car high as a butterfly.

Now one thing that you must understand about the art of mind control from a beast point of view. Is that you never lie to the pray, because for them to be your victim, there has to be a degree of trust coming from you. Thus then, and only then will they allow themselves to become enslaved to you, and to the point of even willing over their life, as well as their soul willingly for you to do as you will; while discarding the flesh unto others to feed upon, filling their needs as well.

As I started to talk to him, in the state of euphoria that, that poison had him in. It became clear to him, that I was a person that he need not fear. However, he could not have been, further from the truth. For long as he was happy, that is all that I needed to destroy and control him. So with that, I continued on with the directions to the *"house of hell,"* where many go in one way, but to come out sick off of drugs, broke, but still alive is considered a blessing. I mean in retrospect, there are those that once they entered, they are never heard of again, like smoke from a fire, they just disappear never to be seen again.

Also, remember by the time we got to the place of his destruction. I had acquired all the information of, his life, and family that I needed to devour him, before spitting the bones to the side of the road. Therefore, in a sense, he had become a commodity, something to be sold for cash or dope maybe even for information.

I mean this really made him my familiar, no more to me than a black cat is to a witch. However, keep in mind that though this was not October 31st, it was still Halloween for him, and though he had not a clue the beast was alive, and riding with him towards his destruction.

Let me see, I guess I could say it was like a good "B-movie," for I was art in motion like a master at work in this field of destruction. Nevertheless, keep in mind that this also, was a lesson for me that would live with me for the rest of my days. I did not know that for every life that I touched negatively, I was responsible for everything negative that came from it and for the whole of that life.

Now this was something that I would learn to refer to as *"A lesson, better left unlearned."* Now by the end of my night as a beast, the sun was rising in the eastern sky as I quickly made my way to the safety of my home where upon at home, I could administer artificial darkness whenever needed. For everyone knows that the beast only find refuge, in the place of darkness thus was my way.

As I sat there in this darkness, the only thing that kept coming to mind was the thought of the next feeding or the next high. For those that know nothing about the ways of a beast aka junkie, understand that it is a life style, and one that needs to be nurtured and fed often. I mean it was not the money, it was not the drugs, it was all about the control, the manipulation and the power over another person's life, sort of like being a God with the power of life, and death in your hands. Yes, I was truly evil and actually at the time, it was not a problem because to me I called it survival; for it was all I knew, and back then it was what you knew that kept you alive.

"Made it, and not a moment too late; let me close the curtains, turn down these lights, lay back, and turn on the television but not too loud to wake anyone up because to do so, would expose what time I really came in. I am home, then like clockwork it happens, like so many times before, the calls of my name which always snap me back to the reality of the presents. *"Kenny Dean, is that you down there?"* … *"Yes, I'm down here putting some things in the wash, and watching TV"* … *"Do you want me to wash something for you?"* … *"No! I'll wash when I come back from work, see you later"* … Thus then it happens, the thoughts of what happened last night disappears, like a case of serious amnesia.

For now the drugs are wearing off, and the mind works over time trying to capture scenes of the activities of the night before only to find that it is lost completely, but to no avail. Then the moment of being lifted up into another dominion takes place, and once again I am in a place a world though parallel, but really quite different, and somewhat pleasing, for it is a safe place. Like the place as a child, you would wish for or should I say longed for so often, but never could find. Now that I am here, it looks, smells, and feels that I am free. However, in the back of my mind, I knew that this was a short-lived freedom, but still freedom at any cost is a welcome thing to me.

The next night again I go out, for the beast is again upon me, and the need is even stronger than the night before, and I know what that means, for I have to find a victim and fast. Therefore that means that I have to get into character and find someone fast. So like a beast again I go into prowl mode, thus once more I am on the hunt. For the need is there, and greater than before plus it is either them or me, for it is not in my nature as a beast too loose!

"Hey young blood is you okay, man where did you take that person you had with you last night? That fool must have spent about, a grand last night" ... *"I took him on a trip to the end of his life, and brought him back so that he can go get more money for the next trip"* ... *"Hell, I thought that you had killed him"* ... *"Who knows, maybe when I've taken him for everything then perhaps I will!"* Look, you know how the game goes; you never let them know who you are or where you live or even where it is that you come from! Because once they wake up and realize that you took them for all they had that is when the real problems start, and that is when it becomes either your freedom or their death that is the time you decide what the outcome will be. That was the thoughts that flooded my mind during those moments when I was on the prowl, and in addition I would wonder why it is that during that time in my life. I was so afraid of seeing my own reflection in a mirror, for even I had a great fear of myself when I was in beast mode, and just the sight of my reflection in a mirror or on any shiny surface was enough to send shivers even through my own bones.

Well as it goes my activities, and the many years of addiction and self-abuse, was enough to cause the break down, and loss of the only real family that I had ever known. This would prove to be the catalysts that moved me towards, actually taking the time to really look at myself. Moreover when I did, I did not like what I saw, I mean it made me sick, and as I stood over the bathroom sink hurling all that was in me down into the drain. The only thoughts that came were *"How can I change this person that I had become?,"* but like clockwork the urge of the beast needs fell once again upon me, and that only made me that much more sicker. Now, you would think that that would be enough to make me stay in and sweat it out; however it was not to be.

For the needs of the beast are stronger, and thus would even supersede the wants of even the master of the body. So like many nights of the past, (though I did not want to go) I found myself once again, on the prowl in beast mode hoping to satisfy the needs of this voracious creature even though this time, I would feed with a vengeance greater than ever before.

However, with my mind wondering and with the thoughts of blame on all those that I felt had did me wrong or even let me down, there was this fire of hatred that burned ever so greater. I became filled with the emotional thought of *"Fuck Them All, For I'll Make Them Pay and With Their Own Blood!"* … Nevertheless though in reality, I knew that the blame lay solely with me even though I hated everyone else for my mistakes, yet in my heart there was this cry out of emotions that I believe somehow kept me sane, as my mind became filled with a plea for hope like: *"Oh LORD, Please Help ME or Take ME Away!"* Over and over, time in and time out, like an endless thought or dream.

Out of everything that I prayed for, this was the one statement which stood out, and in addition I believe that that one statement somehow convinced him of my readiness for change. However that was not to come, for still quite some time.

Now the morning of the next as the sun started its rise in the east, I found myself standing in a park across from a church. Now this was rather unusual, for I was one that did not like to be in the presents of the light of the day or for that matter any light, and the idea of a church, well this I must say could only be a God sent. Nevertheless, for some reason that morning it did not matter, and it felt good, like something different that I had never before experienced. For a moment, I had thoughts of possibly even going over and maybe even enter the church. *"However for what?"* well that never really came to mind, and I believe that was the start of the many times, I would have those feelings and each time they came, they would prove to be stronger!

"Hey Mister, can you help me?" … *"Mister, are you okay?"*…Even though I could hear the person, never did I look in the direction of those questions. All I did was turned and walked away in thought of what a most beautiful day it was. Moreover, the fact that I was

out walking in and through it, was amazing above all. I mean the people, were like no people that I had ever encountered. Perhaps because when I usually come out, they are usually in bed sleep in their place of safety (their homes), though it was like everything was coming at me in 3D. For on this morning the beast walked among the living, and not one of them even recognized me, it was as if they did not even care! That is when it came to me that perhaps I was not the beast I perceived myself to be, and perhaps alternatively the Lord the Deity had stepped in just to allow me the chance, though small yet still a chance, to actually walk among people and to be perceived as liken to them, like human! Now I know that this must sound to you like a lot of bull, but then and again how many of you ever walked in my shoes or among the darkness of the demon world alongside me.

I tell you, in that moment I knew what it was that I truly wanted. Most of all peace was number one on the list, and refuge from the darkness, also from the world that I had so bought and owned property in. For once I had become ready to leave the demons of the night and prepare for something more in tune with what I felt the Lord the Deity had envisioned for me. Yes in that instance I become human, and I liked it and I wanted more, nonetheless it was not to be.

Why, for there was this road that I had to travel, and just to get to whom I am today. Though I must say it was the longest, and the loneliest road that I have ever traveled. But wait; let us not get ahead of the story. For the next thing that came to me, was that I was now standing in front of the home that I lived at, and on the north side of Minneapolis. Now for a moment I wondered how this could be, nonetheless the thought of being like those people that I had just experienced, was much stronger than wondering how I got home. I can also remember that when I walked through the front door I fail to my knees, and in addition I asked the Lord the Deity to find favor in me, and to help me to achieve that one want, which is *"to be like human among the rest!"*

Now between then, and the year 2007 many things happened to me. Things like over doses, suicide attempts, violent acts against others as well as against me, the crying out to the Lord the Deity to rescue me from the hell, and the demons in which I dwelled among and so on.

Then it came, my day of deliverance, and on January 18, 2007 the day that the Lord the Deity saw fit for me. I mean on January 14, which was a Sunday a voice came to me, and suggested that I might go to church. Therefore like a person without power, I began to prepare myself to attend church as I was told to do. Now keep in mind that within my mind, I was still a part of the life practices of my Demonic sibling, and also the laws that govern our dark family, so for the most of my life Church was a *NO-NO!*

Yet and still I prepared myself, and out of the door I went trusting on only the voice to lead me. Now, understand there were two such churches in somewhat close proximity of both me and each other. The one at the intersection of Sheridan and Doweling, and the other at the intersection of Russell and Doweling, exactly a block apart, and I was baffled as to which one I should attend, thus after being ignored by a woman, whom I asked which church should I attend. I again turned to the Lord, and asked the question of him, thus he then pointed me to the church at the intersection of, Russell and Doweling.

Now as I approached the doors of the church, the Pastor Plack who was, and still is the Pastor; came out, and greeted me. *"Welcome Brother Ken, welcome!"* Now understand, some years earlier this same man presided over the funeral, of a young friend of mine. Now, at this funeral there were many people there, who were all Hells' Angels except for three people. They were one Indian, and two Black Americans. However, never do I remember, ever talking to the Pastor or even letting on to who I was among this clan of people.

Thou it was many years in the past, I was still startled over the fact that, he called me by my name, and for a moment it came to me. That perhaps the Lord the Deity was in fact (that very day) walking with me. Sort of like protecting me, from the children of the lost who was, at that very time, calling out! I heard them pleading to come back, for to them my presents was quite important, and to their every being!

However, though I could hear the voices of my desperate siblings, somehow the presents of someone greater in voice and being, perhaps the Lord is who kept driving me towards the door of the church. Now today, I feel good when I say, that I am truly grateful for that moment of support. For without it (his mercy) today I would not be alive, and had he not been there or by my side on that privileged day of my life, this story you might not be reading. A most precise moment, one in which I will live forever because it shall forever remain within me as proof that his existence is supreme, and without question anymore!

For now, my eyes truly were opened, and now I wanted more. I mean you must understand, on that day in the year of our Lord the Deity, and for the first of many days to come. I felt what it was to be free, from shame, anger, hate, shattered dreams, and so much more. For once, I knew what it was to be alive; it was as vivid as a 3D world. Moreover I could feel that my life had a purpose, a true reason for being. In addition, through it all I felt good about myself, and for the first time in my life I truly mattered!

Therefore, for the next few days, I put the life that I was attached to on the back burner and began to apply myself too this new way of walking through life a new journey with the hope of a better life was the prime purpose a life of lesser pain and everything that it breads. Of course, it was fed by the salvation of what positive concepts life, that was still embedded me from the point of my creation, and a hope for a better way of living the remainder of life, became the "new prime directive." So on the night of January 17, 2007 after the night services, the Pastor came to me, and pulled me aside. Then he spoke things to me, things that gave me hope. He then told me, that my destination was one, which would bring me both hope, and peace. Then he directed me, to a building across the alley from the church. Now this I must say, had me quiet baffled. However, like before after sometime over the period of that night, I made a decision. That if ever I was going to change my life, I would have to follow the words of the Lord the Deity, be it directly or indirectly spoken to me.

So on the morning after, with my pride on my sleeves, and my gun in my black leather bag. I proceeded to the place where, I was told to go. Now you may ask, why take your pistol? Well, all I can say is that though my mind was sit on change, my heart still did not trust man, perhaps because of my past, and the things like lies, that man spoke so openly to each other. Moreover, had I not been convinced that the words that came from his mouth were true; then I would (at least) be able to continue life, as I knew it! However this time, it would be to an unusual extent beyond anything, yet perpetrated on the human race, by the likes of me. For on that night, I was prepared to kill, die, and finally be done with the hell that surrounded me.

Yes, I was ready actually to become that demon of death so talked about, but never experienced. I mean that was to be my last straw on this pile of straws, which I had built up around me throughout the years. Moreover, based off what man had told me as far as how to achieve peace, through hope and faith. I mean so much was riding on the conversation of that meeting. In a real sense life or death, truly I was ready to except one way or the other, the end results as the way in which I must travel in life, and with no regret was the mind set at very moment, so as the slogan goes "In for a penny, in for a pound," and I must say my bag of pennies were pretty heavy by that point in my life.

CHANGE, A LOOK WITHIN
THE MIND OF INSANITY

Chapter 4: Do I get a Shot at Life or Not

There was once a time in my life when the thought of life never even mattered. Except in the case of whether or not, I will be able to practice my trade (crime). Now during those days, to me life was great (so I `).

Then it happened, like in a very bad "B" movie. This is where my world was suddenly turned upside down, as it came crashing down all around me.

The next thing that I remember was that first time I saw in the mirror, the damage a shotgun could do to the human body. Then the next thing I remember was, that in my mind I was asking "Do I get a Shot at Life or Not" … Then it dawned on me, that there was no need for me to ask that question.

For the truth was that I had been dead, but for some reason I was back alive. So perhaps the answer was in the fact that, I was standing there in front of that mirror, and looking at a reflection of myself.

Nonetheless, after that it would be some years, and a lot more work, by both the Lord the Deity, and myself before I would look into a mirror again…

When I think about life or the past, one thing is for sure, and that is that the fact that I was murdered, and with a shotgun helps me to keep my mortality in check. In addition, it took quite sometime before, I could even stand in front of a mirror, and look into the face of the reflection. For to me, I was still dead, and somehow unable to except it as a fact. I mean that when you really look at it, there are many levels of death. Levels like the moral death, the physical death, the emotional death. Nevertheless, the most important of them all is the death of the spiritual soul.

Now I can truly say that, of the four deaths I have named, I have suffered them all. Somehow, for me the pain was somewhat the same. For when pain and death becomes a part of your everyday personal life, somehow the pain seems to have no depth. Okay perhaps maybe there is that one that somehow does get to you, and yes, I have been there to, and it always ends up being the worst one of the death that you would dream of experiencing. Nonetheless, there was always something, which gave me the hope to continue. Or perhaps it was because I would on occasions of euphoric transfer tell somethings to the people around me, things that perhaps they should not have known or even been enlighten of, yet of the few people that I ever told these things to, they always somehow gave me an answer. One that always included the Lord the Deity and the love he had for me. Thus, could it have been their fear of that moment, which created this oar or need to be ostracized.

However, then there was this one person, from wench he came, I know not. Nonetheless, when posed with the same question, the answer that he gave was quiet different, and one that made more sense than all the rest. I guess you could say that it was the answer, which I had been waiting for all my life.

To me it was the truth with hope, grace, and mercy all wrapped up into it. Like words from the lips, of the Lord the Deity himself—*"So you want to know, what lay ahead for the likes of you? Well I suggest that you take the time, to study the person in the reflection of that mirror!"* …

Now upon first hearing the response, it somewhat angered me. Then it made me explore the mirrors reflection, which intern happened to be me. Then I put the question to that of the reflection, *"So do I get a shot at life or not?,"* and like magic the answer was there, in the fact that there was indeed a reflection, and it was the reflection of me!

Well from that it became clear to me that until the Lord the Deity sees fit to request my presents, I guess I will continue to have my shot at life. However, what a person does, with the life he or she has is even more important. For it determines whether, you join the Lord the Deity in the next life or wonder around in purgatory. Or on the other hand, wonder until such time he (the Lord), feel that your do a second chance from which, the hope is that you will get it right the next time. Now surely one might ask, what does it all mean? Why such a vivid description, well I will tell you, *"Because life itself, is quiet a vivid experience."*

I mean, when you consider what it is that you have with this thing called life, the only thing left to do is to just learn the word , and even a person of no life experience could and would be amazed. Moreover, the detailed description is a necessary given to the need for change. Thus, this was the moment in which, I knew change was my only recourse, so with that I began to make steps towards this most needed commodity, *"CHANGE"*! Now, understand that for me, this was unknown territory. It was a place in reality that was a no-no even to consider, less even to try. Yet at last, it came to me that though new was different, this was a journey to explore further if I was to in fact, achieve my ultimate goal *"CHANGE"*!

I mean I was betting all I had on this new concept, and for me there was no turning back once I went forward with it. So broke, and with nothing to lose I started that journey into unknown territory, carrying with me only faith. You know the kind that gives you the strength to say, *"I can do it!"* At that moment as the light of the day got brighter, it was like I had been reborn, and in that moment, I truly felt that the opportunity for change had finally came my way.

Also inside, I felt like a true hero; for the shot in life I so longed for was here, and all I had to do was to stick with it. Thus then, and only then for once I would be truly a winner. I could have a real life, and that was all that mattered to me now…!

CHANGE, A LOOK WITHIN
THE MIND OF INSANITY

Chapter 5: The Journey to Change in all its Glory

"As the sunrise, casts it glow upon the road ahead. The traveler, after hours of journeying, could finally see his way clear.

In addition, what he saw was to his likening. For to him, he actually felt that he had arrived at the place that for many years, he had longed for" …

That next day pretty much started like so many before. You know, those days when all you want is to hide under the sheets until the darkness arrives. Like one of those things, you find lying on a slab in the county mortuary. You know like an undead, just waiting to be picked up. Then almost like magic those ideas, and feelings would began to fade. The thoughts of a better life were in my mind, giving new meaning to me. Moreover, in such a way, that it would cause me to want more of this commodity, this new thing to experience this new form of life and living in it. I guess for me, this form of existence was so new to me that it was more like, being inspired by something I never thought could be found in me. Thus the drive, and motivation so bottled up in me, was like being in the euphoria of a fast moving craft. Suddenly I was catapulted, and down a journey towards a positive change in my life, and it felt good.

When I think back to those earlier days, in my change process it was like I was being introduced to new things. Moreover, they were giving balance, and rhythm to the whole structure, and fabric of life. For once I could say, and with no reservations at all, that the existence of the duality of life for me had been proven. I mean, I had in fact experienced the one way, without even knowing of the other's true existence. In fact it was almost like having, a completely new world revealed before my very eyes. In addition, the more I saw, the more I wanted of this new way of life. You know, there is this funny thing about people and journeys, which is that the people on the road of that particular journey, never even pay attention to anything alone the roadside. However to say the least, those are the things that give emotion, to the experience of the "journey." For the things passed during the journey, are significant towards the understanding of the process of change as well as the journey as a whole. Nonetheless in relation to the "from negative to positive change" aspect, plus how it works in that particular person's life along with what can be gained from the experience itself? Now for me, this journey was equal to that of a child in a candy store, surrounded by the many treats, and with my eyes at a wonder. I was taking in by this new view of life as if, "I was inhaling it like fresh air." For me this was that moment of finally being able to, breathe.

Like being truly free from things, which never should have been revealed to me in the first place!

Nevertheless, I was to suffer the same faith as those that went before me, on those journeys of changes… I guess to say the least, my turn around was somewhat quiet swift, and with positive results so far. In addition, because of that fact alone, and knowing what I do about things happening to fast. Well I must say, sure I was somewhat afraid of if the positive results were there to stay. Why not, because the fact is that I am as human as anyone else is. I realized that all humans pretty much struggle with somewhat, the same problems. The only difference is the manner, and way in which they choose to deal with that "said" problem. For the results, be it positive or negative, is what you will receive in the end. Therefore, the manners and the ways are very important choices to make, giving birth to your choice of a positive result.

Now understanding that is what allowed me to see, and with open eyes that the choice's I made in that past life, even though at that time in my frame of thought were positive, they were of a negative way of living making them positively evil choices. Now with the reality of "the duality of life" revealed to me, I have faith that I will try to make all positive choices, and in the positive way of living making my life positively positive or so I wish and hope to!

Now, as I proceeded along my journey, visions of the pass continually plague my every thought. As if the evil that was still within me, had finally put forth the final thrust of its dying army towards the battle, and for better or worse the commitment was made. Even though I fought the good fight and fought to stay sober. It was evident that some degree of backsliding was to be a part of this thing called positive change, and soon "this too I would know to be true." Thus the truth about recovery was soon to be revealed, and in all its glory, for this was the test that I was to either pass or fail!

CHANGE, A LOOK WITHIN THE MIND OF INSANITY

Chapter 6: The Truth about My Recovery, Really!

There was once a man who, for whatever reason, tried very hard to understand the 'Truth' about his recovery. Nevertheless, to great dismay, he found himself lost in the quagmire of his own dismay. Lost to the truth about this thing called recovery, and the process there of.

Therefore, out of despair, he took a chance at the only option he felt he had left, and that was to go with the flow, 'win, lose or draw'! Now, what he found is something that you, the reader, will have to find for yourself.

So with 'no further ado,' allow me to allow you to search, and find whatever truth it is that suits your need. For in true reality, though we have somewhat same or similar problems. The manner, in which we choose to deal with the problem, is the most important thing that we as individuals, will have to do in life, and for the whole of our lives!

As time moved on, the time had come for me to put a sense of 'urgency' towards a full-blown physical. I mean though I knew pretty much, most of the damage that my body had suffered and endured, in my mind the timing could not have been better. Why, because I was (to my knowledge) well beyond the point of no return. I mean in my way of thinking; I was only a few hundred kilometers away from scoring a slam-dunk for recovery. So I thought! Soon that part of my thinking was to take on a new form of thinking. Thus, I found myself at the VA hospital, in an office where I sat in a chair next to a desk. Yes, a desk where so many times, and on any given day you will find the doctor. A person trained in the art of wearing a slight smile, as he tries to convince you that though it sounds bad, it really is not. Nevertheless, in the end it always turns out to be somehow, the worst thing that he could have said.

Either way for him this is only a job, eight hours a day of bad news with a smile, then the pay check at the end of the week. Soon the door opened, and this person in maybe his late twenties or early thirties entered and announced himself to be my doctor. Then taking a seat at the desk, he proceeds to thumb through the documents of a file that he had brought with him, which had my name upon it.

After about five minutes, he turned to me, and gave me the same slight smile, and the same news as everyone else. Bad news, nevertheless, then he looked at me and said, "at least the damages are repairable." Therefore, with that I began to ask questions of what he could possibly do alone with me, to better my situation in addition to acquiring a better health practice, which would add longevity too life and hope.

Now keep in mind, that after hearing what he had to say. I knew that this was not going to be an easy chore. Therefore, everything that he brought to me I studied, as if I were in college working towards my finals, in the field of medicine.

Look! For me to beat this, it was going to take a team effort. In addition, 'my life' is riding on it! So on or about mid-April of 2010, I was introduced to the manner, and ways in which this new miracle I was about to embark upon was to take place. Then that is when, I think my whole world came crashing down all around me. I mean this was the first time when in my life, I had come close to dying, and it was not either self-induced or brought on by crime. Like, for the first time sense childhood, I was experiencing what it was like, not to be in control over your own destiny. Like being nude in a crowd and dying at the same time was the feeling of the moment.

Why, because 'I' could no longer bare the pain of that emotion, or the pain of the illness. I was somewhat faced with the decision of at least trying something, so I forced myself to go to the VA Hospital. Now, though at the time I did not know it, I was only perhaps twelve hours away from death. However, the fact that I made it there, was the thing that actually saved my life, and to 'The Lord the Deity' I give 'the Glory'!

However, unknown to me at the time, this was to be the first part of the miracle or test for my life, which came in like a Lamb only to end like a Lion, in every respect of the meaning!

For I had not a clue, that before it was all over, I would have come so close to death that even the prospect of sleep had to wait. Why, because during that time I was in conversation, and with those who had gone before me already. Also to think that they took the time to come back, visit with me, and inform me while in the euphoria of the pain reducing medications, which they had me on at the time, made it seem yet so real.

"You must prepare" is what they should have told me at the time, for on the first of the year, January 1, 2012, the second half of the miracle or fight for life came to be. Like the old saying, and with a force equal to that of, the proverbial Lion. Now with every progression of the illness, it was as if the light of my life was dimming. However, I could not change it. I mean I can still remember being in a bed, in a ward were all that they could do was, to administer high-level pain pills, and in abundance just to stabilize the pain that I was suffering at the time.

Look, I was dying, and they had not a clue as to why, plus on every visit by 'the doctors' during their rounds in the ward, I would try to convey what I knew the problem to be to them. However, to no avail. For to them nothing I said, ever even mattered. At last, after going through all their possibilities for my condition, it became clear that perhaps maybe the knowledge of the illness as well as its cure was in the words coming from the mouth of the patient, "Me!"

Therefore, they began to listen, and do as I asked even to the point of taking a part of my body and casting it away that the rest of the body might be given at least a chance to survive. I mean had they acted sooner on the information, perhaps the part I had to give for life might have been spared. Then again, maybe it was part of the plan in the test or fight for life. Whatever the case as if it has been said 'in for a penny, in for a pound,' and believe you and me, at that time a pound was a start for me, and a very good start!

Therefore, as they listened to what I shared with them about my illnesses, and the pills that I was taking for them, as well as potential side effects, you know things like the loss of the white blood cells, body energy, loss of appetite, and the breakdown of the complete immune system. Well I think they were amazed, and from that information along with re-reading back notes in my medical files, it became clear that, what I was suggesting was truly the course. Thus as I spoke, they followed; moreover, it became clear to them, that perhaps my knowledge of the problem, and its cure was greater than theirs. I mean face it the concept of, 'a fight for life' was a real thing to me. For at any time I could have been gone, and none of this you would be reading.

Shortly after the operation, it became clear to me that in that moment of humbleness, what really saved me were the children of the Deity, for they had (during my time in that medically induced euphoria), diagnosed my problem, and gave me multiple solutions for said problem. Now I know that might be again a bit for some to swallow but trust me when I say that this is what happened. As I began to heal, there were still problems that I was confronted with daily, but the most critical one of the problems was the loss of appetite. Now if you do not eat with the medication that I was taking, your body does not make blood, and antibodies thus the pill's themselves will kill you. So, as my recovery from the Hospital went on. The body was starving which means, less I do something to turn my *"lack of appetite"* problem around, then I would surely die.

Now knowing this, I began to try whatever, just to encourage an appetite. First thing that I did was to give the problem to the Lord the Deity and wait for his answer. Look, I know how it sounds to you, 'me given control of my life or death to something or someone else, truly not me!' Yeah right! For what is missing, is the fact that though I was changing, no one around me ever saw it? Cause if they did, they would have not frowned, when I explained what was happening in me to them. Things started to happen to me, and for a moment it felt like I was going backwards. Nonetheless, the Lord the Deity, has a way of taking you only as far as you need to go just to get you back on track, also it doubles as one of his ways of testing the faith you have inside for Him.

I mean, I can still hear His voice as it spoke to me, *"So do you understand what your purpose to me, and to this existence is?"* I mean I had to stop, and really look around because in the past everything that he told me, either pointed a direction or gave me an answer. However, during those moments, the idea of suicide once again, did come forward in me however, as quickly as it came it went that was and is a good thing. For now it came to me that whatever power, I needed to make that change a reality was already inside me, and the only thing that was needed to bring it out, was faith, truly just faith....

Hey look! What is faith? Faith is the ability to believe that whatever choice you make towards a positive change, is the right one, and with no reservations or second thoughts. For you already know that the answers come from the Almighty, and that is a good thing. So as I had done prior, I continued with the newly found faith that so far had gotten me thus this far, for I had no bad reasons or thoughts not to.

As I recall, on that night of the call to the Lord for help, there was much concern as to was it all worth it. I mean the completely second shot at life thing, and if I could go through the sickness any longer, for it had come to the surface this sense of doubt. Like there was this side of me, that was saying give up, and die. But there was this other side, which kept me focused by saying, the answers that your seeking are just beyond the horizon, and you can make it just one more step that is all one more step! So with that I continued on, and a good thing it was that I did. For today I am still here, and loving every bit of it, in pain or not!!

Now as you all well know, just when you think that the end of the road is close. That is when like clockwork, a curve somehow always appears where one should not exist, and yes this was the case for me, a reality check just to let me know that this was not going to be as easy as I had perceived it to be. Truly, this would be a lesson worth remembering, and one never to forget. For it had come to be that regardless of how hard I tried to put distance between me, and my past, it was going to be harder to achieve that distance than I had imagined.

Never the less, the beast once again tried his hand, and once again it was calling me back into the darkness. For the urge of that need was once again upon me, and with even greater force than ever before. It was as if it was putting all that was left in it towards the utter and most complete destruction of all my possibilities for a most positive change in my life. Now for a moment I must say, I was almost com-paled to give into it like so many times in the past. However, the strength of the faith that I allowed the Lord the Deity to manifest in me, was like a neon sign flashing *No!* So again with the help of the Lord, this beast I would beat back and hopefully for good!

Well the year is now 2012, soon it will be 2013, and I am starting school soon for two reasons. First, to understand what occurred in my past that put me first on this journey, a road I call the road to hell, and destruction, which will help me to better understand who I really am as a creation of the Almighty.

Secondly so I can learn how best to help others that they, may not have to bare the pains of the past as I must do. If there is any irony to all this madness, I guess it would have to be that before you or anyone can past judgment upon anyone, you first must place your feet into that persons shoes, and then walk down that road traveled by the person. Thus then, and only then you will know what lies in the mind of insanity based solely on what you see, along the roadside of that person's life. Well I guess that this is the part where I enter that most awaiting statement of morality, thank you for your time, and ask that the Lord the Deity shower you with both blessings, and favors.

However, unfortunately all that I can offer at this time is the truth, by going further to say that if you feel that you still have any remnants of what is perceived as morality, left in your every fiber of being. Well I suggest that you look deep down inside and work very hard at pulling that to the surface. Why because to change is not an overnight process, it is an ongoing life practice, which will be with you for the whole of your life. Therefore, without further ado let it be so, and keep the faith…

~Foot Note~

L ife is an experience that puts you, if allowed to, right in the mist of what the Lords plans are for you. I guess in some ironic way, it's the Lords way of telling you through your insanity, and trials and tribulation of living that though you are not perfect, he is still there for you, all you have to do is reach out or call out to him.

Even when you think that there is no one listening, call out or reach out, for he is all seeing, and all knowing. If you just have patients, he will reveal all the true wonders of the world before you.

In addition, the secrets of the whole of creation, he will bare before you. A Universe of Wealth and Knowledge to behold because that is his purpose, moreover his promise to you, along with grace, mercy, and because his love for you is that strong.

So with that do yourself a favor, and trust in your faith. For that is all that you have, and that is all which it takes to be one with the miracles of life.

Again thank you and peace be upon you all,
Kenneth Bernard Dean/ LDD/ SIX (Author and Scribe)

CHAPTER 2

"Council before the Great Almighty on the Subject of Man"

~Author's Word~

D uring one day, a long, long time ago, predating the dawn of "the man concept" by about a thousand millenniums, the day set for the council to meet once again came. Thus, like the rest of my colleagues, I too made prayer and then did (in fact) attend. However, what you are about to read is an actual argument and-or discussion from such a meeting, which in turn was about the importance of, as well as the purpose for the "man concept" and what it might mean overall too all in concern.

I mean when you consider the fact that though the design and DNA might differ somehow. The overall concept had been tried and had failed many times and on many Worlds throughout this vast Universal existence. Yet, in a sense, what could or would have given us the confidence to believe that with a few tweaks, perhaps too the structural design and also the DNA. Maybe implanted the idea that we just might prove to be successful or bore perfection was (in fact) the basis of the argument. Moreover, how could we be that naïve to believe that it could even work after so many failures thus far?

Nonetheless, the fact is, this was a task set upon us. This problem equation: seeking a positive result in the end and is given to us to solve by the Great Almighty, the Lord God himself. We hoped that we might develop a working idea for at least the structural design and a new DNA concept in this meeting. An idea, which (indeed) we might be able to present to him for his final decision. Now, whether this will be ideas and concepts, which he will use, one only knows. Yet, at the time, this was our only purpose and one that would be till the end if need be!!

So, once again, we find ourselves journeying down that road of both investigative discoveries and exploration by way of those elusive memories of my past life before man. And in search of the truth of purpose for man, which in some ways might prove to be quite shocking. So, without further ado. I give you the piece titled "Council before the Great Almighty on the Subject of Man." I also hope you both take from its clarity an understanding of its purpose and great interest to ponder later. Moreover, I would like to thank you, the reader, for your time and interest in my works.

(A Peep through the Cracked Door of a most Heavenly Meeting: From the Book of Six)

"Council before the Great Almighty on the Subject of Man"

There is something which I now clearly remember from my past of long before man even existed. But what stands out more is something which I heard, and while on route to a place within the hallowedness of the presents of the true Deity, the Lord God the Great Almighty. I remember as I walked in grace, along the grand boulevard of gem in-crested golden pavements, which lead to the Great Chamber of the Great Almighty, at which point, often we would come to meet before His presents.

Something fell heavy upon my ear and caused a significant pondering to occur on the day's meeting. It was as followed these words "I did hear," which perhaps is the reason for my every being, as well as my existence here:

"The fact that we have tried many times over, and on many Worlds throughout the vastness of eternity. Yet only to time after time again, bring forth nothing but failure is truly the sum to this problem equation. Truly, He must know that there can be neither compromise nor any solution to this problem, which we so have been tasked with for the pleasure of Him alone."

"Surely this must also speak to the lack of necessity for such a concept. I mean, are we not enough, and even with our own imperfection. Surely, "He" must know, we both love and worship "His" every existence." "Clearly, we must have fallen short of his favor, or perhaps this is some sort of a test for the pleasure of Him alone, do you not think?"

"Does it really matter Ezra or are you all forgetting that this is the Lord God, the Great Almighty whose love and favor is being questioned here. Have we forgotten who and what we are to Him so that we feel or think we have the right to pose such questions on such a matter? For, it is my understanding that our purpose is to serve his every will. No questions asked! Moreover, not to do so will only lead to falling out of both His grace and His favor. So again I ask you all, is this something you truly want to continue pursuing?"

Little did I know that by hearing this, would put me among the many test specimens to which, would inherit this thing known to be called the "Test of Trials and Tribulations." It has long been said that loose lips sink ships, yet what is not said is that an open ear will bring forth an unimaginable journey of unique experiences, coupled with a rebuilding of strong faith in the true Deity, the Lord God the Great Almighty. However, this is a thing that I hope you will determine through this piece.

I can remember that there was a moment of question, which came upon me as I went forward, and along the boulevard of gem in-crested gold pavements, and into the Great Hall of the Great Almighty. This was the place where we would often come to meet in the Great One's presence on matters of his choosing. As memories present themselves correctly, I can remember that the atmosphere was one of the significant concerns on both the hearts and minds of all in attendance. For, when last we came together to meet. We left with a feeling of failure for not having solved the problem equation, which had been set before us by the Father the Great Almighty himself.

Yet, in a sense, there was this moment of revelation or feeling inside me, which led me to believe that this time, things would occur during this meeting that would bring forth both clarity and an acceptable end to this madness of seeking a reasonable sum or solution, to this unsolvable request or problem equation handed down to us, this *Council of New Designs and Ideas*" members.

For, even though the atmosphere was thick with the arguments of purpose for this concept *Man*, and (also) equated equally with ideas of how best, if need be, to accomplish such a task. There was still a sense that this time, perhaps we would be able to achieve our goal at last. I mean, as I think about the situation again. It becomes clear to me now that our purpose was to do all we could to give the Lord what he was so requesting of us, which at the time was our only purpose. No matter how long it would take or how much we argued over the purpose or reason, we were there at the pleasure of the Great One, the Great Almighty himself. As memories do not fail me, I recall the conversation in the Great Hall going this way (so as), to give you the mood-feeling of the moment:

"So again, yes, Jacob! As we find ourselves once again here trying to come up with both a purpose, as well as a reason for this new thing or concept, Man. Nonetheless, coupled with determining how best we can solve the problems of such an idea given to us to solve. Now, are there any suggestions?"

"Well, my brother's, first of all, I don't see the point in it. This new thing, which is called Man that is. I mean, are we not good enough for our Lord, the Great Almighty? Have we not every day worshiped and praised him in the manner requested of us? Is the Father not pleased with us any longer?"

"I'm in some ways sure that he is. But John, the nature of our Lord, is to create on a broader scale. For that is what "He" does, and our job or purpose is to assist in making it happen for the pleasure of Him alone, no questions asked!!"

"Therefore, I pose the question again, and to you all, are there any suggestions on how best we tackle the task at hand?"

"Well, brother Ezra, I suggest that whatever we do, we don't give them the complete package of senses that we have been gifted with. For to do so would probably defeat the purpose set for this new thing. This Man concept, which is so desired by the Great Almighty."

"Okay, I can agree with that Jaydan, for it is a fine idea. Now, does anyone else have anything more?"

"Well, brothers, even though I'm okay with that aspect of the base design. I still feel that it could prove to be somewhat a cruel way to exist. So, I would like to go on record with the suggestion that we at least, though not giving them the full array of the thirty-nine senses. Let us at least consider giving them the five basic ones. You know, the ability to see, smell, hear, feel, and speak. The reason is that they will work well with the choice and free will options, which will be implemented later into their DNA mark-up, or do you not all agree?"

"Yes, brother Otto, I agree with the giving of the five senses. For, to give them more will make them liken too us, like lesser gods. Also, remember that this is just a prototype for the amusement and pleasure of the True Deity, the Lord God the Great Almighty. And who can say that he will even consider this concept anyway!!!"

Having argued that point successfully, the conversation moved swiftly to physical body design and dual or singular gender identity. Some felt it would be better that [they] should be hermaphrodites. The reason is that on other worlds, we've had a lot of success in both the concept of the "A-sexual" designs and their ability to maintain a balance.

Yet, what we failed to recognize, was that on every one of those worlds. There was no diversity within the humanoid population that inhabited them. Moreover, there was no diversity of any kind among any of the different concepts that coexisted alongside them.

For, in that instance, it became clear to me what the Great Almighty was seeking to bring to both our creative minds and all viewing eyes. Which was the one thing that gives power to the art of creativity; this thing we now know to be called "*Diversity*," and what a wonderfully beautiful concept additive to the art it was.

For it gave purpose to the idea of creative thinking, as well as design. It also brought forth an array of new shapes and colors, never before imagined by any except the Great Almighty Himself.

"Now that we are settled on giving them nothing but the basic five senses, how best then do we proceed on a base design, or are there any suggestions?"

"Actually, I think that we should use the number five as the design base, somewhat like a star's five points. Okay, hear me out on this, for the design should be one that is both unique in the concept of being basic. Yet it should depict somewhat, the image of the Great Almighty that all who lay eyes upon it, shall be humbled by the very sight of this new concept. Thus, they will know that it is of the Lord thy God that it does exist, this concept Man and like before in His (Own) Image!"

"Now I ask you, is this not a good and noble thing to do. I mean, can this be accomplished with the use of a dual-gender concept, a thing never tried before?"

"Yes Ezra? What of the dual gender situation. And what will that say about the Great Almighty to those who will question the gender of This Great Almighty in the times to come? How do we control the focus of these concepts thinking, so that it does not cause problems to the flow of their belief towards our Lord?"

"For, I to concur with Jacob and the question posed about, what we can do, to offset their thinking after once it is said that they are created in the image of this Great Almighty. Will they believe that the Lord is both Male and Female? And if so, how do we correct this prior to production?"

"Well, my brothers,' I suggest that we write into the DNA, the formula for shared responsibility. Look, we give them both male and female responsibilities, which will only work through compromising and working together. We also implement in their minds and hearts that the Lord God, the Great Almighty, is both the Supreme Creator and Lord of Lords. Now, by doing that will take away the petty thoughts my brothers, of whether or not the Lord is either male or female. Sort of like in the end, does it really matter that much when eternal life is truly the goal. Thus, the only concern then is to believe and have faith, and do you not all agree?"

A healthy suggestion indeed brother Otto, and one which I feel strong on returning to at some time later before the final discussion is made."

Now, upon hearing the argument and or suggestions towards these new concepts, design ideas. It became ever so clear that unlike prior concepts and ideas, perhaps we may be in over our heads. For this, one task just might prove to be the most complicated of all. I mean, the very idea that it was to depict the image of the Lord God Almighty; meant that the uniqueness alone would bring forward an array of complications unlike never before.

Thus at that moment, I felt a great fear come upon me as to whether or not we were on (at least) somewhat the right path for such an endeavor. Then I looked up towards the bright light which sat upon the throne, which (in fact) was the Lord God, the Great Almighty. Now, there was this calming peace that washed over me for a moment, as I could feel the view of his eyes fall upon me, and in both my mind and heart. I heard these words in the form of questions, and a statement that came to me from Him this Lord of Lords:

What is it that troubles you so? I have been watching and listening, yet from you, not a word has come. Yet, on your face, there is a look of despair. Surely you can tell me, can you not?"

"Dear Lord God, the Great Almighty, it is not despairing, which troubles me. But fear for creating ideas to a concept, which will depict your image. Moreover, coupled with this new dual-gender design concept for both male and female, and how best to accomplish the accomplishable while at the same time pleasing you. Because my only purpose is to serve you only, and in whatever capacity you choose. Moreover, that is the purpose of us all, for your pleasure alone. Yet, I'm afraid of not being able to birth perfection by way of imperfect hands. Understanding fully that this is what you are seeking from me, and I can't afford to give you anything less than that, perfection. Yet how do I do it without compromising my place in your favor?"

"Listen my child, do not be afraid. For, by the close of the meeting, I will bless you, and many liken to you with an answer to your problem, but in the form of a request. Therefore, do what is asked and worry no more. But do remember what I ask of you, is merely for my own pleasure as well nothing more nor nothing less."

Needless to say, hearing that was like the lifting of a million tons of worry from these frail shoulders, and I felt blessed for the reassurance gifted to me at that moment. However, what I or any of the others did not know at the time, was we were going to be the first, after the creation of man, to actually take on the test of trials and tribulations full swing. Doing so would allow us to feel somewhat what it is to be a prized concept of the Lord God, the Almighty, and later to feel the power of his judgment.

I mean, who best for the job if not, those whom the task of design and idea was set upon for them to accomplish. Sort of like what a cook does, when he tasted his cooking first, before serving it to his guess or perhaps when a massive automobile manufacturer test drives the new automobile design before marketing it to the consumer.

The good thing about this thing is that as the cook with his extra salt or the automobile manufacturer with higher quality and safer seat belts, we also had tools. We came armed with both *"free will and the option of choice,"* the two most essential tools to have. For, from these tools comes faith, humbleness, sacrifice, belief in the Father and His power, and the full understanding of pride and its purpose.

Yes, the more I looked at it, the more it became clear to me that this whole thing was more for understanding and for learning than anything. And in the hope that we might be elevated to the next level of existence, which is *"Creator Helpers"* or simply *"Lesser Gods."*

Considering the fact that if you pass the judgement, then the next position after favor has been granted, would be to create in the name of the Almighty God himself, along with the full knowledge of right and wrong. Thus, allowing you also to be able to assist or take on the task of judgement if asked to do so. But I'm getting a little too far ahead, so let's put the brakes on, and get back to the piece, okay?

As I can recall, after that so-called moment of Revelation reassurance, I gestured to speak. None-the-less, I was given the floor. Now, as I stood there with this newly found confidence, my obligation to speak was to our own benefit. For, I soon understood what the Father meant in full. Therefore, these are the words, which found their way into the hallowedness of the Great Hall:

"How can you know that the answer to the problem is the right or true answer if you've never been vexed with said problem. Thus, forcing you to go through a number of the options in search of the most right or fitting answer or solution to the said problem?"

"So, what do you suggest would be a fitting way to solve this dilemma?"

Then a loud voice equal to the sound of a herd of large, hoofed mammals, perhaps five million strong, rolling ever closer from afar spoke these words, which was and to this day still is the LAW:

"Lest they suffer pain, how then can they know relief or how can [they] determine what is good if they know not evil?" Thus I say to you all and before eternity. Because they have chosen to go against the word of the day, this world gifted unto them is now surrounded by sin. Therefore, all who come in it from this point on, goes into it by way of evil. So let it be written, so let it be done!"

Now upon hearing the voice and words of this Great Almighty. The vastness itself illuminated sounds of Great Praise, liken only to that of perfect pitch wind instruments saying only this:

"The words of this Great Almighty is both Just and the Law. Blessed be those who will take on the test of Trials and Tribulations, for they shall be called the children of choice, and the children of the Lord God the Great Almighty!"

"Now it is my true understanding, that this task or responsibility we have all been gifted with, is a thing that we will come to not only know but experience a great deal through living fact."

"Explain more, my dear brother Six!"

"Well, my brothers and sisters, I don't feel, think or even believe that it is my place, as well as the will of the Lord God, the Almighty that I can do that. For he has blessed me with the encouragement that in due time, all things will be made clear to us all. I mean, are we all not here for His pleasure alone, and if so, then who are we to pose such questions of this matter and at such a time as this."

"Yet brother Ezra, I will go on record to say that what we are all about to embark on is a thing far greater than we could ever imagine. For, it is of the blessing of God Almighty that these favors shall be gifted upon us, and I believe that we shall and will do well with it. Yes, in some ways, it will seem somewhat mind-boggling. But those are the times when all our faith will be tested and tested it will be. For, to completely solve the problem equation put before us to solve. One must live through every step of the solution, to both feel and understand the problem as it is being solved!"

"Again, dear brother! I ask that you explain! For that which you speak of seems to be that of riddles and blasphemy. Thus, I find no reason to listen any further to such nonsense!!"

But before I could elaborate further. A bright light from the throne of the Father, the Lord God the Almighty. Came upon us and manifested itself among all who was present at the meeting, and in that moment any question in need of an answer was in that time answered. For, that was the moment he chose to introduce to us, his concept of the *Test of Trials and Tribulations*, coupled with the tools "*free will*," and "*choice*."

Now, during this time, there was utter quietness. Followed by the mighty sounds of praise and rejoice, signaling the end of this "*The Council's Meeting on the Concept of Man*." Why? Because after hearing all that was said within the meeting, and byway of the Lord thy God. A decision was made by the Lord; that it would be better that we become the living concept of man. They were allowing us to fully understand genuinely the reality and the complexity, of the living existence of both our design and our ideas for the man concept. Now, though, some will find this hard to believe. Still, it poses questions as to what must have occurred when the idea of the man was ever discussed.

Now, if that is the case? Then I say to you that the piece has done what it was meant to do, which is to raise a reassurance towards your faith and belief in the Lord God the Almighty. So with that, I say, thank you for your time and may the Lord's blessings and favors always be upon you.

~FOOTNOTE~

There is something which occurs in the minds of us all, when confronted with the reality of a more powerful entity or should I say the Lord God the Almighty. In most cases, it can be consider as being fear. For, though the entity is of a tangible nature. Still, the fact that it is not of a physical nature or form is what drives that said fear. Therefore, it becomes somewhat shocking or frighting when actually he reveals himself in your presents, even for the so-called believer. But it then becomes reality in a sense, which alerts you that you've made that final crossover from this reality. The one which you've so become comfortable with living, into this new one that you have no past knowledge of, which is the true nature of this said fear.

But understand this! For that is what we here all signed on for, when the question was posed to us all long before birth. Or at least the remembrance of our accepting to take on this, "Test of Trials and Tribulations." Are we not like all those before us, and those that shall follow us through the final journey towards judgement. Thus, the fear is a thing that we will all have to confront. For, it must be, to complete the cycle that will give documented facts in solving or perhaps acquiring the answer to the question of the real purpose for the Man Concept, as well as humoring the pleasure of the Lord thy God, the Almighty.

Moreover, in the end it is the will of this Great Almighty, which we are in the service of or too that we are here. However, there are still those who are always ready to jump at the chance, to bellow out in loud words "BLASPHEMY!" Yet, to those I can only say still those words, lest you find yourself an open mouth fool before the glory of the creator, the Almighty God and true Deity.

For, it is written that these things shall come to past, and what is written on this day is the actual truth as it was and is. So, be not afraid, for the road we walk; is the road we all signed on for. And the only thing which should be of concern, is the faith you have in that which created us all. That which we know to be the Great Almighty, the Lord God. As always, I hope that the peace "Council before the Great Almighty on the Subject of Man." Posed reason for you to ponder your faith in the Lord God, as well as soften your heart towards your fellow brother and sister. For, in the end that is all that "He" wants from you.

Again, thank you for your time, and may the favors of the Lord God the Almighty, cover you like a warm blanket through a cold winter's night…

Kenneth Bernard Dean/LDD/Six (author)

CHAPTER 3

"It is, what it is!"

MY QWEST FOR CHANGE, AND
A BETTER WAY OF EXISTENCE
~Author's Thought~

"**S**ome things never change, for the way it is, is the way it has always been…"

That is what continued to play throughout my mind as he sat across from me and tried to find dignity in the act of a lie that he was about to impose upon me.

But you know, with me being me and knowing that the end was at hand, the only pleasure that is left to me (a survivor of a lifelong war of these illegal acts), was to watch him shrink deep into himself revealing what he was, the demon and a living lie.

Knowing that it is not the way of one liken to me, to believe in the lies of one liken to him. Well I must admit for a moment I almost bought it, but thanks to the actions of those like him. For they were not to let him forget who he was, and where he came from and forced his hand to act in accord with the agenda, and laws in which pure evil exist.

Now to them and their acts of lies and deceit, all I can say is thank you, thus the evils of man go on like always. There is a saying that I wrote in a book that I left in the corner of my room, in the dimension of time and space that only Gods and the children thereof exist in, and it read like this: "To see or hear evil in its purist form, has been known to change even the likeness of GODS, and their children thus the clans of evil grow to be greater. So, remember that before you believe in someone's words or action's, you have an eternity to study them. Before you choose what, they are offering, you need to know that you have options. For they need GODS and the children thereof, to give strength to their existence not us. Thus, we are who we are, and they are who they are."

Thank you, Lord Deity, for without you I would be liken to them, like demons. For they see me as weak thus they should know that; that is when I'm at my strongest for I am SIX, and they exist for my pleasure only, not the reverse.

And in the times to come they will know me as father and fall down on bent knees with the mark of my number upon their heads, and upon their lips my name shall be burnt. Thus, low and behold these things shall come to past, and they will know me as LORD!

I am their Lord SIX (LDD)

Now, as it comes to past, there was a time in my life when the lesion of evil and I was one. For they were many, and they were in and a part of me. Thus, when I walked, they walked, and when I turned, they also turned.

Then the favor of the Lord, the Deity, fell upon me like that of a great and mighty force. Thus, revealing to them that I was of this great creator; [*that*] which created both time and universe.

"*Now, when they saw this, they fell before me, and said these words;* "*Please! Oh please! Do not destroy us, for we want what it is that you have acquired. Oh please lead us to the Deity, so like you we might stand in the light as well?*"

But, the Lord, the Deity told me to not move fast, for there is lies in what it is that they ask. So, with that in mind, I took a step back, and looked at the situation once more. And like it was told to me, the lies I could see.

Again, thank you my Lord, for keeping me in view of the truth over that of a lie. In other words: "*It is what it is, and though you may not like it, you still must live with it. So, in truth, GET OVER IT!*"

~Foot Note~

The reality is that to pray is likening to, having the blinds on the windows opened and revealing for once, the light of the true truth. As it enters, bathing the darkness with both its warm brightness and truth of enlightening wisdom.

The prayer: "Old Great and most powerful one, you said only through prayer and belief can one only achieve the blessings and favors of the Kingdom of Eternity. So, for that I am truly grateful, thank you for hearing me and coming to my rescue."

Kenneth Bernard Dean/LDD/SIX (Author and Scribe)

CHAPTER 4

"The Art of Life"

~A word from the Author~

It's not like I don't know the internal struggles suffered by those close to me, it's just the idea that they fill I don't know or even understand it all. Yet in true fact or retrospect it is because of me, that this thing or reality is. Now whether they don't know of this information or the fact that they do, and still refuse to accept it, thus allowing me to lead is what the real issue is.

For to stifle any forward motion within me, is to condemn the all, to some degree, yet even till the end, my full commitment is to the sacrifice. Even at the cost of my life, meaning not just the life you know within your own true reality. But the one true reality, "you know," the one which allows me that responsibility. For in the time to come, even you'll fall before the truth when confronted with it.

Thus in that moment it shall finally be exposed, and even then! "I'll still show love, for everything flows downstream, including and especially true facts!" Whos' facts? My facts, for if it's not about me, then how can it ever be of or about you! Now I bet right now, what is going through your mind is one of two thoughts? The first one being of a spiritual ridicule, which in some way is more in the design of requoting the words of the father; but while forgetting the reason in the first place, and the gifting those words actually bring. It's like they refuse to accept that this is my test of trials, and tribulations. Thus if I win we all win!

Then there are those others. You know! Those people who become violent, both in words as well as physically. Never even giving thought to the whole prime directive set before us all, and the consequences for the ramifications, of their uninspired action, and in the direction of the sin known as, "the refusal to accept the truth sin." Do they not know the full meaning of or the depth of what it truly is like to inherit birth byway of sin. For the world after Adam and Eve, was forever to take on a whole new set of rules. Do they not know that the rules, which govern all options and choices, were forever altered?

Therefore, both your burdens will be heavier, and your faith shall surely be tested; thus I pose to you the question of: "Do you really think that when you're talking, and I'm nodding my head. That I'm really either listening to or agreeably paying attention to what is actually coming out of your mouth? Well the truth is, when it comes to you, I'm not!"

For the truth is the word, thus only the word has that power of forgiveness, which is truly needed when going through a thing such as, "The Test of Trials and Tribulations!" Yet I ask that you walk side by side with me, as together we go in search of the truth. Also again I'll request that we walk together in a state of open minded awareness, seeking only the truth. For that is truly the one common fact, which breeds substance into this reality; so with truly no further ado the piece, "The Art of Life" and as always I hope you both enjoy and take from it, something of importance to ponder.

"The Art of Life"

Perhaps it may be appropriate to say, it is apparent by now that you, who follow my reads. Do in fact take the time to actually ponder some of what you read. And still there are those, who just read it as a way to justify some of the sins they perceive, they can break. While in the hope of achieving a set point or position in life, when at such a time, they can find the purpose for leaving that life practice and pursue one more befitting someone more faithful.

But either way, it is good that you do read them. For it's my purpose, to arouse that thing in you called question. Thus is the purpose of all, and any who scribe. Prophets, proclaim to know the truth, Seer's or Watchers give vision into words of what is yet to come, and that to have purpose. But the purpose of one who scribe, is to bring forth the message in words, and in the way they are received by said scriber, "That a word might fall on ears, seeking opportunity in search of and for the truth."

It has been said that the true reason for purpose is twofold, first thing is that it builds a dedicated faith, and the other is, it gives a reason for the passion in life itself. For to be without purpose is that of nonexistence and living without purpose. Though this is not a sin, yet in a sense to some degree, if you look back upon it once more, thus even you would see it as a sin of a sort as well. However enough with that, for I feel that the point is made. Thus surely even you can see, and do understand the complexity in which, I think through the problem or equation put before me.

Or perhaps your thoughts were of a more primitive nature, thus not allowing you to comprehend even the base of what it is, was or going to be, which I'm trying to convey at any given moment. And that is okay to. For the right of all is that you can take the time to decide on a choice. Because once the choice has been made, all that's left to do is the following through with it. Good or bad, it don't matter once the choice has been made, it becomes a fact, one of those un-excludable fact, yet another course or route to the journey in your life is added. Though we all will have, on an individual level, contact with many other individuals (more than you can even keep count of) is not the question. But what did you gain from it or even give to it to enhance the shared moment or to replenish the value of its properties! You see, this is the very things that we are all guilty of, the inability to accept, and build on the information freely shared among us all. And for the betterment, and future of humanity as a whole; yet there is that time when we all have had that one ah-ha moment. That moment when through our own ideas and words, we were able in conversation, to for once speak the truth. Be it about faith born situations or just everyday life, yet only to be shouted down by the nay Sayers.

Painfully crushing, I know. How? Well because, this is a thing which I've lived with; and for as long as I have lived among the moments, and situations of this reality. It knocked me off my square for a while and had me lost to the dark side in question as to why or what truly is the purpose of my existence. However, as I sat there in shameful wondering question, as to the purpose for me. A voice came to me and freed me from that dark place.

A place which I had become content with, for the voice itself had the strength to both lift me from the darkness into the light, but more importantly it restored me to my set purpose. It also reassured me that in the end, I alone am responsible for the actions of my life, no one else! So whatever I do, do it in the name of that which created us all, for only he can forgive, only he can make anew that which has become old and ugly. With a whisper he speaks, and life exist wherever he commands, and in whatever shape or form of his choosing. Then in a very loud and demanding voice, these words he spoke into me: "*I'm the God of Abraham who went on to through Moses hands; deliver the children of Israel out of Egypt, and into the land I so promised to them. Thus I say to you, that the purpose you serve is at the pleasure of me alone, thus till such time your work is done you will scribe the words that I will impress upon you, that they will know them, thus they will know you as well."*

Now what is it that I just said? *"You will scribe the words that I will impress upon you, that they will know them, thus they will know you as well!"* What that means to me is for me to not care too much about what others might say, once they've read what it is that I've wrote or dwell on what they might feel about my faith because in the real sense that's personal; hence, *"A personal relationship with the Lord thy God the Almighty, the one and only true Deity!"* So I guess for me it is a little hard to hear the words spoken by people who refuse to make those necessary sacrifices, which they are trying so hard to drag out of me. But all the time overlooking that the true problem, lay with them all along. I mean when you really look at it closely, you'll find that the first option is to self, and then if there is any who has an open ear, the opportunity is then open for you to do your thing to help them into the light, less the brow beating manner so used.

So till such time presents itself, if you're a Christian, I would think that you would look differently at those around you, and in a more accepting manner, rather than just another person headed for Hell. I mean when it's all said and done, not all who profess to be strong of faith, will be among the first round draft picks somewhat, if you get the meaning. But then who am I or better yet what am I that would speak such words of wisdom? Someone just like you who understands fully what the end game brings, so why should I listen and believe all that you say when you have less power over my life than I do. I mean when you really give it some thought, even you might be surprised to find out that maybe I do have a little more power than you. And will share it, but for what reason this time do I make the sacrifice, is it to be used and kicked to the curb once more.

Hey look, I can't afford to spend the rest of my days, asking the Great Almighty to give me another shot at a purpose when already he's made me aware, and again back focused. Again I say, show me a miracle then perhaps you'll have my ear. But till such time, my purpose is to serve at the pleasure of Him who creates. The one we all know to be the Great Almighty, the Lord God, and the true and only Deity. So what is "The Art of Life"? well it's this unique thing in the way you live life, like a painted master piece a true original, abstract, personal, again unique, but all so lonely. For in the end, judgement comes to us all individually, so I can't answer for you nor you for me thus in the end we are all yoked with it. Like our own personal yoke, do you not agree? Hence we are all individual works of art, master pieces of the Master Himself, AMEN!!

Okay perhaps you're a little vexed by what it is that you've just read, and in some ways I sympathize with you. For you're still young with your awareness and lost to the words of man. But I always pray for you all, and before I pray for myself. Even though you might think the worst of me, I mean, what law states that all but me can change, and if none exist then why the treatment as if one does exist, and only you know of it. You know there use to be a time when once I thought that it was okay to be that way. Why, because it showed strength and power over others, but really what it was in reality. Was a form of belittling those seeking words of truth and wisdom. Thus it became evil in a sense to me, and my way of thinking was then elevated by the Lord God to take heed of that choice. For in the end, we all have to answer for our action and do we not?

I mean I had to come to the conclusion that in the end, the only one that has need of the facts of my change is the one who forgives, and if he's happy then so too am I. Thus I pray that that be the case for us all or if need be, I am willing to sacrifice that it be the case for all, less myself if need be. Even though I feel that, when it comes to me, no one would even entertain a thought such as that on my behalf. However what happened is that there was someone who felt that I was worthy, and who did make such a sacrifice in not just my behalf but on the behalf of all from the beginning, until, and beyond. For him, the son believed in me and before I ever even existed, and he is the one who, I owe allegiants too. So what you think, or feel don't really hold water to the fire in his words, for you pretty much are like me, no more no less just is. But what does matter and is true is that I work for him, not me or anyone else, it is him alone and in whatever capacity he demands.

So like I said before, it's about me going through my on test of trials and tribulations, and even though I know this, my worldly experiences I still struggle with. For that is my test, those are my trials and tribulations, which confront me throughout this struggle for my salvation, and to again be one with the Great Almighty. I know that there have been times when even I would silently scream out, that if asked again to take this on, I would keep my mouth shut. But in the end, we all know that it would never happen. For when he ask we respond, and why because he is Lord of Lords, and God the Great Almighty, that which created us all. *"Also we do it because it is of the pleasure of him that we all exist, and can there not be a greater reason, yes?"* As of today there shall be an even greater change from within me, one that will allow me that peace to go forth with what it is that I have been sent to do. Whether you understand or not, there are words that must be scribed, that you who might read them will find purpose through thought to make changes that will make a difference in the world. For in the end that is all that is required, and who knows, perhaps it might work for us all. So don't be alarmed if, I am different in a sense through my words scribed on paper. Because it's the will of the Lord God, that this thing I do, and till such time as he stops the communication.

So in the future keep this in mind, when confronted by a written piece from me. For in true actuality, the words are from him believe it or not!! As always thank you for the time you spent reading the piece "The Art of Life," and I hope that in some small way, you have a better understanding of life after awareness of the truth. For the piece, like all the others, was meant to cause question and thought of all who read it, thus bringing forth the birth of freedom in a sense, again thank you.

~Foot Note~

For this "foot note," I feel it necessary to focus on a word that so often is misplaced, misunderstood, and oh so often misused. The word is "Repentance," and the reason is perhaps because once we inter in too this life by way of sin. The fear of being alone, and without the visual presence of the Lord the Almighty God, left us as individuals lost. We became selfishly caught up, in a never ending struggle to recapture that place we once held, within the warming light of the presence of the Lord God once again. Thus from my experience with members of the human concept, it too; can and will affect you as well, and in more ways than you can ever imagine. Why? Because it is in the nature of humanity, this self-preservation clause; this need to in the end stand and bask in the light of the Glory of the Lord, thy God, once more. But this time for the eternal ever, like it started out to be before the concept of man was ever conceived.

Yet we all find ourselves in this struggle, and because we agreed to take on this Great mission for the pleasure of the Lord God. This great fact finding journey in search of the truth or should I say the true sum or final equation towards solving the concept of man, and the problems that comes with this new concept. Now remember that before, I said that we were sent here equip with tools. Thus I spoke of two such tools, one was "Free Will," and the other was "the Option of Choice." However though these tools were gifted unto us that we might use them, with the hope of finding our way back to our creator, the Lord God the Almighty. Yet the true reality is, it was a designed catch twenty-two situation or scenario set up to see if in fact, we would be able to choose the right tool, when the time becomes necessary that we make such a choice! Therefore, we were gifted with the option to ask to be redeemed, and through our ability to ask for repentance or simply to repent. Moreover, in doing so, one can and will be redeemed, so is his promise to us all. But how can that be, when so many refuse to see in others what they so say, or claim is in them. For to fully be of a redeeming spirit, one must also except that what he does for one, he does for all irrespective of the sins being repented or even the person who's repenting.

In writing this there are two things which comes to mind, the first being that "God so loved both the world as well as humanity, that he gave his only begotten Son that they might be forgiven and return to him once again. But this time eternally, thus forever standing and basking in the Glory of His Light eternally. And the second one is the definition of the word "Repentances or Repent":

REPENT vi, vt. To feel remorse or regret; to change one's feelings about—Re-pent'ance n.—re-pent'ant adj.—re-pent'ant-ly adv.

Now, in the reading of this definition, I can't find any statement that speaks in a sense only to or about you, does it not speak to us all as individuals as well as the whole, does it not sound like a gift for us all to use towards redemption? I mean when you really look at it, I find great sorrow in being the one to bring forth such truth, which you now have to except, in fact of this thing we so know and call "The Art of Life."

Despite the consequences, when you truly look at this thing we call life or the living of life, in most ways it is like that of painting a portrait. A Master Piece worthy of bringing before the Almighty God himself with each brush stroke where it should be, a canvas of perfectly pitched hues of unique quality gathered together through the use of the tools of Free Will, the Option of Choice, and truly the main ingredient, the ability to Repent. For it is truly in us all to create a Master Piece, which is the Spirit or Energy that we call the Soul; something that we all have, the thing we must return to present on the Great Day of Judgement, and before the Lord thy

God, the Great Creator of all things great and small along with you and me.

Now, in keeping with the set course, it is okay that I suggest from the point of an artist; that we all must do all we can, and most importantly, for those who are trying! Whether it makes you feel good or not. For the trueness of the Master Piece, which in fact is you; is not so much in the work that you do on self, which makes it a Master Piece. But the work that you do in others, the pain that you can understand of others, and the acceptance that you show towards what another individual profess to you of the changes in their lives.

Why? Because that is in a sense, the only true purpose, which we all share. This job of working a Master Piece into the souls of the others lives around you, is in itself, what creates in you the true Master Piece that is worthy of presentation, and before the Lord God Almighty. In any event, I would like to thank you for the time you took in the reading of this piece. Also I hope that perhaps you took from it, something worth pondering as you continue your search towards, the truth of "The Art of Life" again thank you...

Kenneth Bernard Dean/LDD/Six (Author and Scribe)

CHAPTER 5

The Man Name SIX

~Authors' Word~

There comes a time when we all ask ourselves questions like "WHY ME?" and "WHAT'S MY PURPOSE, AND PRIME DIRECTIVE?" For years this has been going on, and with no change other than the person that is asking. Well, with that in mind, then you know, I also have pondered these questions. Not just once, but on many occasions.

Only this time, I asked these questions in writing, and onto you, the reader. So with no further ado, "The Man Name Six" …

First off, allow me to introduce myself; Hello, my name is "Kenneth Bernard Dean." However, the name that was given to me before birth is SIX. Now, some might wonder, "*What does he mean, before birth, the name given to him was SIX, and why?*' Well, unlike many of you, I was gifted with the knowledge of who I was, both before as well as after my birth into this world. Thus, for quite some time. It has caused me a great deal of problems, and while trying to fit into this reality. Therefore, I cast myself into that never-ending cycle of going about the day to day struggle of fitting in or making do with what was available. My first encounter with this dilemma was the acceptance of my place, in the color scheme of the society (in which) I had been so boldly cast into.

That had to be right after I became aware of my existence in this [my] newfound reality and understanding fully that time was at hand. Therefore, from the jump I knew that my hands were full, and there was not going to be anytime for handling this mildly. Yes! [This] was going to be quite a job, both in retaining prebirth information and keeping true to the prime directive, which had also been set in place for the job at hand! Also, for the longest, I've had this deeply embedded belief or knowledge that, indeed, "I was born Hebrew."

That in itself somehow puts a twist (even more so) into the equation. Why? Because most equate Hebrew's with being Zion's or Jewish. But the truth is to be Hebrew; you can be of Arab or Zion/Jewish culture. Meaning you are defined by what Deities' hand designed you or the tribe you belong to and their beliefs as well. I, on the other hand, follow no man or his ideas. For, I talk directly to the father, and he talks back to me as well. Thus, I come straight from a Hebrew Deities hand, who you know as, or call *"Yahweh the Almighty."*

To understand the statement *"being created in the image of the creator"* is to be created with the same blood as this significant entity, and from the same flesh as well. Thus the blood, and flesh is that of the actual Hebrew. So in all actual actuality, we are all of the blood and flesh of the Hebrew. This creator of the universe, the worlds, and all that exist within this incredible vastness. So, whether we like it or not, the truth is always the truth, which is truly the painful fact of it all. I mean, to finally have to accept the concept we are all from the same hand, and that that hand is Hebrew; should not be hard to swallow, though for some it is. For they have been taught, to be Hebrew is to be Jewish/Zion. Yet that is truly a lie; *all praises are to the almighty "I AM," from the beginning, until, and beyond amen!*

For the blood and flesh of everything that ever existed, be it of the past, present, or future. If it came from or will come from, the hand of the Lord the Deity. Then, without a doubt, it shall, and always will be, Hebrew! Though, as I said earlier, *"I know that for some, this might be a hard pill to swallow. But, the fact is that this world, this universe, and all that exist in it is of a Hebrew existence and is of the mind of a Hebrew designer. So we [like children] inherit that from our father somewhat, and that is the pure truth. Like it or not, so get over it, okay?"*

Now there are those who believe in some form or way, that I'm either a fool or crazy for saying or even writing this. But, to them, all I can say is the time for them, and their understanding should come sooner than later. Because then they will know what it is that I know and feel. Thus, we will both be on the same page about this Great Creator of the Universe and its worlds.

So, with understanding all of that. I continued on with the seeking of whatever is left of my prime directive, hoping all along that it will keep me focused and on course. Plus, within the direction which I should be traveling. Also, in line with the belief that I will complete the mission, that is mine alone.

However, as the sun hit the sky's mid-day position, my surroundings' sounds come alive all around me. In a sense, like the planet, and all in it was talking to me and me alone. As all the world's flowers released their fragrance or the language they use to communicate with each other. Thus, at that very moment, both enchanting and enticing me, with the sweetness of creation. This scent of their favor.

In the distance, the animals and birds' sounds called out to me in the name, which was mine before birth. For, they know of whom I am, along with whom the Lord our Father is as well. So to you, great father, thank you for blessing me with this reminder of your love and power. This [in itself] lets me know that your favor is all around me like the soft blanket [of a newborn]. Heated by the warmth of your love, grace, and mercy as it keeps me warm, through those moments of chill. Which I have encounters with so often in this my journey and task. Or then and again, could this really be curiosity about how well I will fare in this my dilemma? Now, as you read further. You'll understand why this statement is so crucial to my story.

As the day grows old, the night comes upon the sky like spilled ink on white paper. Soon the heavens are covered throughout with these grains of diamond dust. Sparkling, and flickering in the darkness of the heavenly sky, known to me as the night. The sun of the day has been replaced by his younger sibling; we call the moon or Luna.

As I lay on my back looking upwards into this masterpiece, it is like staring into a living fresco ripped from an Italian wall of the past, and cast high into the heavens. Yes, for this in itself is nothing less than a gift, and of that who created us all! But the question that I ask is, was this ever meant for my eyes, or is this just one of the perks of being here in this reality, and upon the face of this rocky world we know to call Earth. Or perhaps the gift is one that was meant solely for the pleasures of those who were created with the same flaws that befell me?

Whatever the case, the beauty of it still is true and heavenly. Now when we consider this thing, the prime directive. It then becomes reasonably essential why we must take into consideration the purpose of it.

That being, all things must continue its course, and without any distractions. Not even the slightest change in its flow, for if (in fact) this thing does occur, then the whole purpose of the individuals' being would be lost. Now, if that happened, and without any course correction. Then that person's goal becomes of no great value anymore. Thus, the individual's life continues, but without reason or purpose!

In the past [many times], this has happened, and it has always led to the destruction of many entire civilizations. So this is why it is so very, very important. That we all look into ourselves and force the remembrance of both our purpose and our prime directive to which we have been charged with.

However, when you realize that you were considered damaged goods from the start and knowing that the cat is now out of the bag. Well, it has a way of forcing your awareness of the uniqueness that is you, and that by itself should give you your purpose at least. Thus your prime directive becomes '*to live life to the fullest*,' so to read further into this piece should prove to be quite interesting, so let's continue, shall we?

'*How can you tell when you've located both the purpose and the prime directive?*' This is a question that many have asked, and the answer is as follows; *they represent a way of living (purpose and prime directive) rather than a thing that you can see, smell, touch, taste, or even hear. The objective is the purpose for living; the prime directive is making the right choices when confronted with an option to be made.* So it should read as follows: *'living life through making all the right choices or at least half of the right choices.'*

When you read it and put thought to what you have just read, it somehow seems impossible to *'live life by way of making all the right choices or at least half of them,'* unless it truly is a perfect world. You see, had man not took it upon himself to deceive other men around him, and then force-feed them the concept that he was the living God, thus training them to believe that they must follow and obey him. Well, things perhaps might have been different, or then maybe not! Maybe the Lord (the Deity) wants us to struggle, like hoping that it will make us stronger and immune. Yes, immune to those deceptively, distasteful lies that those other men have in waiting for you. Well, at least, that is how it is with *ME!*

How about, we just reflect on the subject at hand for a moment. That being the purpose and the prime directive. But only for the sake of argument, let's look at it in a more personal view. I mean, like in all great stories, there is always a subject, a purpose, and a prime directive. Well, to the surprise of the reader of this piece, I have to admit that I'm the subject, but the purpose and the prime directive that was once mine, well, all I can say is that they somehow are long gone. "Where?" Is something, which I can only try to figure out. Perhaps through digging deep down inside myself, pretty much like I have been doing for most of my now sober life, is probably where I'll find the answer.

Look, this is a process that feels like trying to dig through real granite with just bare hands and broken nails. Indeed an insane decision, one that I don't think another would be fool-hearted enough to take on. Meaning, *'nobody but me that is'* plus it only applies if (in fact) I was really meant to be. Also, we must consider the characters that live in this reality, on this world, and in the time we all live through. Now in doing so, I guess the only way to describe it is to call it *'True Insanity'* or *'Hell on Earth,' for man's ways are of violent war, hatred, deception, greed, and all things vile and repulsive.*

For these things help him to know true goodness, and to understand what it is, to be able to go to the Lord (the Deity), and ask him for forgiveness. He also thinks as well as says that this is what the Lord Deity wants us to both do and be. For it gives him something to do, rather than just spending time lying around on a cloud and causing thunderstorms, another of his believed past times! To hear me say or write that for you to read would have you both saying and looking at me as if I was crazy. So I say consider if I was really meant to be, at least before you think or speak.

But, come Sunday, the pastor of the *'Church of the Hood'* can say it, and not only will you take it in with an occasional "*amen.*" You'll even pay him for those lies and carry them home to share with those that could not make it to the service. Plus, you'll call it *'being a good sane Stuart of the Church!'* Now, let that just simmer up there in the dome for a minute. *I mean, after a short while of kicking it around up there, it becomes clear that for all those years, you've been treated like an idiot and played like a banjo in the hands of the town redneck, at some back-water jute-joint, south on plantation road, down in hang-um-high Township.* Now, when you give it a second thought, it becomes even more apparent that the only thing you have to do is to follow the Ten Commandments. Also, to dig deep into yourself, seek your real purpose with a smile on your face, and a song in your heart and keep your faith and belief in the Lord strong!

Now this is coming from something, which came into this world flawed from the start, by way of my escape from heavens own recycling bend, and through these things that I have exposed to you, it somehow makes' me feel that there is perhaps a chance for me to have a purpose. But like all things, it's also in the hands of the great one, the Lord God Almighty the true Deity, for I believe that the Lord God helps those who get up and put forth the effort to which I'm doing.

Plus, also remember, *'nothing ventured, nothing gained,' and for those that still want to do nothing, question nothing and even follow like sheep because you feel that it's safer! Realize this, what and who you think is 'Good, and Godly Men of the Lord' are actually wolves dressed in Armani suits and Stacy Adams shoes with a Rolex and a smile! You can tell them from all the rest because they like to use the words 'Brother's and Sister's' a lot.* I mean more than a lot like every other word.

Plus, they are the ones who truly have lost their real purpose and their prime directive, thus replacing them with the task of trickery, lies, and deception, which is all geared towards stealing your life by stripping your purpose, your prime directive, and replacing it with false hope. Then, of course, there's me, the guy who just wants to find his place in this world of chaos and do well with it. For the truth is, I was genuinely hopeless up until my great escape.

But, as I sit here on this grasses knoll staring out into the world, and looking for the answers to my life's problems. I somehow feel like a stranded hitchhiker on the side of the emptiness road, the place where dreams never come true. A place where suicide comes quicker than your purpose for being there, and well, no one even cares one way or another, now that truly is the fate that will befall you, so it came. Yet knowing this, I still stay true to the course and purpose for my being there in the first place. For, to me, we are all flawed some more than me. Now, I think this is why the great one has tolerated me so far and for this long in life.

Even though I [myself] could be just as deceiving as the good pastor, I chose to give myself an alternative way out of this madness. I don't feel that it would be the just thing to do, and it would only add to the pain that I am now suffering more or less. Plus, the damages of those who would suffer from my words of deception (I believe) would be too much for me to carry upon my soul as well.

Someone once told me that if you worked hard enough and prayed every day, then miracles do come true; you just only need to believe, so I do, 'oh how I do,' and even in that, there is a purpose.

There are times when I'm just contemplating or just praying, and then while looking up into the heavens above, the sight of something coming closer forces me to fix my eyes on it. Like from the hand of the Lord, the Deity, both my purpose and my prime directive, seems to becoming ever so close. But then as I focus a little more, it becomes plain to me that like so many times before, it's just a stray bird looking for his home flock which days before went south. So then, and again I find myself like so often, looking for the positive in it all. But to no avail, thus I begin to doubt what it is that I have set out to do. *Questions like, is it all real this life that is, and am I doing all that is humanly possible to find my place in it, this life that is?, Would this world and all that is in it, indeed be that much (more) better without me? Or is it true that my purpose and prime directive is really not life, but DEATH!*

Now keep in mind that this is not just some strange thoughts of a man gone mad, by way of the sufferings of insanity, for this is how I've been the whole of my life here, and to try to explain in depth would be to mind splitting even for the doctors. But there are two people that, on occasions, I do allow them to hear some of what it is to be in my mind. But without letting them feel, through the complete and complex depths of my pain, what it is to be me. That is something that only the Lord the Deity and I can know of. You know, sort of like the truth of the mistake in creativity is out, but we still try hard to keep some kind of lid on it.

That being a lid on my state of mind and the lost purpose and prime directive, which I am so desperately working on seeking, even though the Lord the Deity recognized the flaw in the time of my creation, and decided to recycle my energy into something else. But only after it became clear to him that it was of no great rush (my recycling that is), and could wait till later the Deity took a break. Thus only then could I see hope and perhaps freedom from recycling; you must understand that the Deity taking a break was all the time I needed to escape, so that is what I did.

Thus that is why and how I came to be; I guess that is why the Lord named me as a number instead of a properly worded name. I mean, could it be that perhaps me being here is a mistake. You know, like a real bad experiment that escaped and fell to Earth, which is what I did, and before I could be recycled, and into something more positive like the other five before me.

"I mean that by itself would give a reason for the name being in the form of the number "SIX," and along with the lost purpose, and prime directive things which are the two things I had not received yet." Why, because I, through my escape, changed his plans.

Just say for humor that my real purpose was to be recycled into a more productive life form; well, the prime directive then becomes my complete destruction.

Thus the raw energy could be used to create something more positive. But, when the Lord the Deity saw that I had escaped, he saw me as a unique and most exciting project to behold; therefore, it was because of my strong will to exist against all the odds that guided his decision. It also allowed him to see if the flaws in all that he thought was so perfect could, (in fact) be removed and replaced by true perfection that which he was seeking in the first place.

So along with this great yearning for a life beyond what even he could imagine, he allows me to exist. But, existence without a purpose or a prime directive is equal to that of a customarily created living being. But it is also like being among the walking dead because your reason for existence has not been recognized. Plus, those things' like purpose and prime directive, which turns out to be central to life, have been distorted.

Even now, I feel like my time here in this world seems to be coming to an end. Kind of like a flame on a match stick, and the winds of time standing in wait to blow whatever life in me out, just like the flam of that match. Soon I find myself asking, the only thing that will be left of me in the heart and mind of the Lord the Deity and that is *once I have been taken by the winds of time back to the void of time, and space to wait for recycling,* what is the purpose for the name Six? Or is there something more, which I did not yet recognize; *"Something that was of Purpose and with a true Prime Directive?"*

~Foot Note~

Though I might have many names, the one thing that stands out is that I was created without purpose and without a prime directive.

Now that I must say, it is the hardest thing I had to come to terms with. But that's okay! Why? Well, because I have character, charisma, plus I am filled with knowledge and love. Though there is a design flaw in me, it also works towards my uniqueness, and amid a storm on a starless and black night, I'm the brightest light that you will ever see. For I am Six, the most significant flaw the LORD the DEITY has ever allowed to escape, moreover, from the recycling room in that particular place we know to be Heaven.

Whatever the reason for this thing that occurred (this so-called Paradox), either the Lord or I have not the knowledge or even understand anything other than its necessity overall to creativity. Yet because of it, and through it all, I hope that it gave the LORD the DEITY great pleasure. So if that is the only 'Purpose' for my being then, I will consider that to be my greatest accomplishment; thus then my 'Prime Directive' has also been served.

Yes, for I am 'The Man Name SIX,' that was the name given to me by the LORD himself. Plus, I am his gift of light to you as well, for I exist in that place in the Heaven known as Delta. And I have earned both my star and my home there in the Delta section of the heavens.

Now even though you might not understand it just yet, someday you will, and on that day, we will be as one, and for those that have not, however, comprehended what it is that they have just read. I suggest that you go back and start from the beginning. But this time, take time to understand what it is that you're reading. I mean, don't be afraid to go at it with an open mind, for a closed mind only breeds no knowledge at all.

Like a fruit tree without fruit is how I see some of the Lord's creations, and what good is that to anyone, especially a fruit lover? There comes a time when you have to accept who and what you are, and the place in that life preset for you. So if you do that and stick to the plan, it (Your Purpose and Prime Directive) will not be hard for you to find and follow. Okay, maybe this might be a bit too much for you to ingest right now, but I employ you at least to try to remember your time here in this reality, in this world, and this universe. For the time is fast running out, and before you know it, 2012 will be upon you and gone. Then, that is when it becomes TOO LATE, though life must go on. It will because that is the correct order of things till the Lord the true Deity the Almighty sees fit to put the thoughts of our existence to rest, thus then, and only then will we be no more. Again thank you,

Kenneth Bernard Dean/LDD/Six (Author)

CHAPTER 7

"*True Salt*"

~*History and Insight*~

"S alt," the wealth of a man, once was measured in the amount he held or owned of this fine and great commodity. For when the great and most powerful Lord Deity gifted upon man this most richness of minerals, he spoke it into every being with these words, "you are the salt of my creation." But they (man) overlooked his meaning and used it as a form of currency.

Thus he would pay a man for the hard labor of a day, the wages of a measure of salt, and to the troops for their participation, and survival of a long and heroic battle, the standard of a fifty-pound block of salt was given them each, and this was good. But in actual actuality, this proved to be a bit too much when it came to banking, and heaven forbid that it should rain before they could get their pay home or to the bank.

So with that [man] decided that perhaps, they might look for something else and that something became gold and for many reasons, one of which was the luster of its bright hue, for they saw it to be magical and again the feeling was that this was good. But through this piece "True Salt," I hope to touch back on perhaps what the great and most powerful Lord Deity meant when he spoke.

So with that, sit back and prepare to be enlightened through the reading. I only hope that you (the reader) might be tempted to openly ponder what comes from this read, and come to whatever it is that makes you comfortable by understanding the true meaning of the statement "True Salt" …

After five days of labor on day six, the Lord (the Deity) knelt down and performed his last miracle of the week, before his first day of Sabbath, and into him the breath of life he gave with a blow of air from his [own] lungs.

Upon seeing his miracle come to life, he then looked over the lands of the world that he had just completed and spoke this gift into it by saying:

"Into this great creation I give the miracle of the wealth of this great salt, that it might cover and tame the whole of it."

Thus the day of the six was complete, and on the first Sabbath he rested among this, his greatest wonder and joy; peace and slumber were his comforts.

Now, I can't say truthfully that the Deity gave names to the days that followed the Sabbath and how we know to call them. But on that first morning that followed the eve of the first Sabbath, and as the Lord the Deity open his eyes, the first sight he was greeted with was one of great magical wonder. First, there was this magical place Eden or the garden, and it was accompanied by the smile of a loving man child who at the time (with his finger), was tracing the lines of the face of Greatness in amaze and wonder, and when he (this man child) saw that the Lord's eyes were open. Like children typically do, he rose, and with laughter and joy, he ran away as if he wanted the Lord to partake in a joyful game of catch me-catch me.

Now to see this brought quite a smile to the face of this Greatness, this Lord of creation, this Deity and so much that the first morning that followed the eve of the first Sabbath gave him much joy, and that was the start of the first good day.

He then spoke into this man child being, the ability to with some degree of work, create things of beauty like flowers; also trees of flowers, and fruit as well as the ability to (through the power of touch), bring forth comfort and name to those creatures that also existed in this world of miracles and wonder. Thus as the man child ran and with each planting of his foot, the gardens of the world were created thus the more this game of catch me-catch me they played, the greater was the gardens of the world, and by the end of the day after much play of this game, the Lord and his man child both gave into each other with laughter and joy.

Now, while the father and his child embracing each other, looked over the lands and great gardens that lay before them. The father looked at the child as he held him up high above all things great and small, and to him and before the whole of this incredible creation these words he then spoke:

"For on this day and throughout eternity you will and shall always be known to me to be the TRUE SALT!!"

And the world and all that was in it was with joy and knowledge of the real reason of that statement, thus as the sun went down on the day of the first day that followed the first Sabbath eve, the second eve was born and as the Lord and his man child took to slumber, he the Lord said this is good thus the term *"goodnight"* came to be as well…

~FOOT NOTE~

I t is not easy for man through much time of being taught and led to believe wrongfully, the meaning of the Lord the Deity's spoken words. For overtime, man became accustomed to both the word and the importance of the word "deception!" That being to deceive or to mislead by way of lies.

So for all this time, he never considered or even explored the true meaning of the word "SALT" or even the statement "TRUE SALT," and as the Lord meant the understanding thereof to be.

Thus, is the reasoning for the gift of the piece, "TRUE SALT," which is (in fact) so humbly given to you (the reader), by the next son [SIX] or as you know me, Kenneth Bernard Dean. Though many may deny the historical exactness of the piece, as being true, it is of no importance. Particularly at this point and in these times.

CHAPTER 8

"What is the Price, for Life?"

~A Word, from the Author~

Why is it so hard for a person or persons, to stay true to the agreed upon arrangements, which were agreed upon at the beginning? Therefore, rewriting what soon will be the future and one based purely on deceptive maneuvering, as a form of establishing their place among the rest. Yet, in the wake of it all, they loose sight on what it is; that is at stake! Some call it, "the greatest gift ever, from the Lord God the Almighty." However, just to keep it simple, we will just refer to this "great gifts" name as being "Life!" Yet, there are those who would sale that "great gift" away from you and do it right up under your wondering eyes. For even man, in the close of his reign upon the surface of this world Earth; has out done himself, when it comes to selling the "big lie" to the complete population, the world over.

Furthermore, never looking at the price in consequences, owed for such deception and lies. For in a sense, I guess you can say that it is okay to destroy things or concepts, which belong to you and you alone. However though, to destroy concepts and ideas of someone else, well that to me is just plain wrong. But to take, and try and apply that same form of deception, lies, and trickery to what the Lord God, the Almighty has through love created, and for "His" pleasure alone. Well, I must say takes true hate, and a lot of envy to try and pull off. I mean, do they not know that the "Lord God" is both all knowing, as well as all seeing to? Thus, we again find ourselves in search of an answer to the madness of Gods greatest creation; and byway of a journey through "the mind of insanity" and asking only one question. That being, "What is the Price, for Life?" So without further ado, I give you the piece ("What is the Price, for Life?") and like always, the hope is that you will enjoy it along with taking something of importance to ponder later...

While sipping on a cup of French Dark Roast and toking on a Churchill length Honduras Dark Leaf cigar. I was amazed by what (in light of this man made pandemic), was sent via the internet for me to read. First and foremost, this COVID-19 thing is not a virus, but truly a man modified bacteria, designed for two purposes; one purpose is for population reduction, and the other purpose, as a wartime weapon! Now, what was so disturbing is the fact that this whole scheme was implemented in the order to force the implantation of a chip. Pretty much like tagging livestock before slaughter, in order to have complete control or simply the feeling of Godlike power, when making decisions [in a sense] for the whole of mankind. I mean, did not the Lord God, the true Deity gift upon us all two gifts: free will and choice, asking only in return that we recognize "Him" as the only true "Lord of Lords, and God of Gods, the only and true Deity." Furthermore, did "He" not say that our faith in the earlier statement, even faith equal to that of a mustard seed size, was all that was required to open the door to "Him!" Meanwhile, behind closed doors, man was (for a longtime) working on a way towards replacing this Lord of Lords and God of Gods. And through the use of another gift that came from this great Deity, that being the gift of technology.

For, he (man) thought that if he could harness the knowledge of logistics, and the mapping of the binary concept, along with building a machine capable of applying at a high speed, the use of this binary code or map along with the code for logistics imprint. That they would be able to finally have the power, to challenge the Creator, the Lord God the Almighty. Thus, hoping one day to replace this great Deity, to wit place himself (man that is) in the position of Lord and God. Yet, I say to those men, be not surprised of the end results, for this is a thing, which you have brought upon yourselves; be it by way of direct action or through the support of such actions, seeking to capitalize on the outcome of this venture. Never even considering the consequences, which comes by way of such acts of disrespect towards [That]; which with love and favor to an idea, that being the concept of humanity or simply man! And through the command of three words: "LET THERE BE!," brought all that is into existence.

Then I say to you all: Be mindful of your [naïve character displacement], for this displacement is the total opposite of the one known to be called or referred to as "Common Sense!" Even more, like the aligning of the hands, on the face of the clock of true time. The last chapters of all the books, and of every religious denominations is fast coming into alignment with those same hands, on the face of the clock of true time; thus signaling the ending days or time of man's reign here on the face of planet earth. I mean, from where I am standing, and the view that I have overall of this situation. Well, I must say, it really do not look good for humanity, lest they redirect their focus back to [That]; which with three words of command, gave life to a pondering concept, the concept of "humanity or simply man!"

It is a known fact (that) there is something truly wrong, when the cultural format of the word or spiritual worship, is now an item to market, like so many pairs of shoes. Yet, those who lend ear to such deception and misuse of the true word. Stand barefooted and lost to the lies, and deception so forced fed to them by these evil and vile men and women, who seek also to put a price even upon your own "Life!" And then there are those who come to you under the disguise of false-hood, promising things too impossible to deliver. Thus, again you find yourself once more, caught in the web of deception and lies while these so called men or women of the cloth (they who are looked upon, as scholars of theology or messengers of the true law), by way of lies and manipulation of the true laws or word of the book. Are fast destroying, the opportunities gifted onto humanity. Things like this world Earth with its many diverse concepts, and also theology. Which, in fact, is the study of true spirituality; vastly reducing their view, in the eyes of [That] which created all things great and small, as well as the concept of a vast array of humanoids leading up to, humanity as well!!

Nonetheless, it is a known fact that humanities ability to show empathy, and byway of their actions. Has sat them upon the road to total, and utter destruction. Yet, they find themselves or feel that they are to far beyond that point of return to ever return to any form of normalcy. Like they just do not care anymore for either eternity with the Lord or the freedom of life eternally!! Or could it be that they are simply, to naïve and filled with so much envy towards the idea that they (themselves). Are but an extremely small part of an entity, more vast and greater than they; concept of what is to be, and byway of three words: "LET THERE BE, and they were!!"

Yet, they continue on believing that time is somewhat in their control or that they like a bacteria will (through their conquest over technology) somehow defeat the Lord God the Almighty and place himself on the throne as Lord and God!! Like, who throughout the vastness of eternity would even consider such a thing, lest it be man, the prize concept design of this entities creation. Do they not know of the consequences, which await one so naïve, and dead sat on such a task?

Still, there are those who stand barefooted amongst the fields. Spiritually seeking words of spiritual guidance back to [That] who with thought and a concept, gave birth to their ever existence. Trusting these vile and deceiving liars, with their future gift of eternity with [That] which gave birth to their existence as well. To those individuals I say, be not fooled any longer. For the Lord God has favor for you all. Moreover, the power and abilities to achieve this most sort after eternity with the Lord God the Almighty, lies within you all. Also, the concept of blind tangibility is a true concept, and a thing more real, than one can ever imagine. Begin to channel your energy toward a higher frequency above level 4.5 to level 5 frequency: thus, allowing you through your subconscious state. To fully relate with [That] known to us all as, The Lord God, The Almighty and one true Deity for your answers…

~Foot Note~

It is said that when one or more come together and speak in spirit of the Lord God and [His] purpose for this creation Man, along with this gift Earth and all that it beholds. There is no mention of a price for such conversation, byway of the Lord God, who in fact created all things both great and small, including Humanity as well. All that [He] ask of us all is that we have faith of his existence, love for each other. And the will to be enlightened of, His eternal love and gifts for us all. Thank you for your time, and my hope is that you both enjoyed it as well as took something of importance away to ponder later…

Kenneth Bernard Dean/LDD/Six (Author and Scribe)